The Curate's Guide

The Curate's Guide

From calling to first parish

Edited by John Witcombe

CHURCH HOUSE
PUBLISHING

Church House Publishing
Church House
Great Smith Street
London SW1P 3NZ

Tel: 020 7898 1451
Fax: 020 7898 1449

ISBN 0 7151 4016 7

Published 2005 by Church House Publishing

Printed in England by The Cromwell Press,
Trowbridge, Wiltshire

Contents

About the authors

John Witcombe is Dean of St John's College, Nottingham, where he has responsibility for training those preparing for ordination. He has over twenty years' experience of ordained ministry in a wide variety of church traditions and social contexts.

Diane Clutterbuck is Training Director at 3D Coaching using a facilitative training style with clergy at all levels, which incorporates training theory, theology and spirituality. She was formerly CME Adviser for the Diocese of Oxford.

Vanessa Herrick is currently Director of Ministry and Vocation and Director of Ordinands for the Diocese of Ely. She has wide experience of both parish and cathedral ministry as Reader and priest, as well as having served in Cambridge as Chaplain of Fitzwilliam College and Tutor in Pastoral Theology at Ridley Hall.

Claire Pedrick ACC is Coaching Director at 3D Coaching and is a work consultant to clergy at all levels. She also works with curates and incumbents who are facing a change of direction.

David Runcorn is Director of Ministry Development in Lichfield Diocese – a job that includes running the training programme for curates. Prior to this he was a vicar in West London before becoming Director of Pastoral Studies, Evangelism and tutor in Spirituality at Trinity Theological College in Bristol.

Eileen Turner is Director of Extension Studies at St John's Nottingham. She has many years' experience of both parish ministry and adult education, including a period with the Lichfield Local Ministry Scheme where she trained the diocese's first Ordained Local Ministers.

Margaret Whipp is a minister in secular employment and a theological educator. Previously a Vocations Adviser, she is currently Director of Practical Theology for the North East Ecumenical Course.

Introduction

You may have picked up this book because you are thinking about your future, and wondering if ordained ministry is for you. You may have picked it up because you are already in the process of selection or training, and are wanting to know more about what's in store! You may already be ordained and looking for a tool to assist you as you reflect upon this life in which you now find yourself.

This book aims to help those considering ordination in the Church of England to understand something of what they feel they may be called to. It is for those already committed and in training, to know a little more of what they might expect, and to be able to plan, and pray, to make the most of it. It is for training incumbents, to remind them what ordained ministry looks like through the eyes of their new colleagues. It is for any in the Church who are sharing in reflection on how to develop the Church's ministry in response to God and the world in a rapidly changing culture.

We will start with the experience of calling, selection and training before moving on to examine the life of a curate, with some survival strategies to help with all the changes and challenges of a new and demanding role. In the middle of the book you will find a key reflective chapter (Chapter 4), where we explore the 'being' of being a curate and the ways in which identity and relationship are affected by ordination. Emerging from this, we will develop a series of suggestions for how to develop and get the most out of your curacy as you prepare for a future in ministry. (Those of you familiar with the Pastoral Cycle model of practical theology will recognize an application of that model in the structure of the book, as we follow the reflective spiral of experience–analysis–theological resonances and resources–plan of action.)

Contributors to the book include training consultants, practitioners in ministry, and those who have been involved in theological training and reflection. I am especially grateful to Vanessa Herrick for her editorial support in this project. We hope that this will offer a balanced and holistic reflection and resource for the Church's ministry today.

John Witcombe

1

Vocation, discernment and selection

John Witcombe

There are many forms of ministry. Everyone who is a church member has a 'ministry' – a role, or a part to play, in the life, ministry and mission of the Church. Some see the beginnings of a recognized ministry in a Christian life as early as baptism, others think it starts at confirmation. Whether 'officially' recognized or not, any response in faith to Jesus will involve a call to live a new life – and part of this new life will be to play a part in the life of the Church as it witnesses to Jesus in the world.

Discerning the role to which we are called is an important part of maturing as a Christian. There are many excellent books to help with this process, and it cannot be seriously undertaken without consultation with a local church community and its ministers. The particular calling to ordained ministry needs to be seen within the context of the kaleidoscope of all the possible callings upon the lives of Christians, all of which are necessary in order for the Church to fulfil its calling to be the Body of Christ.

'I don't know if this sounds crazy, but have you ever thought of being ordained?'

It is often friends or family who first suggest ordination – but recognition of a call to ordained ministry may come in a variety of ways. My own call to ordination crystallized in the middle of a stewardship sermon. As I listened to the preacher speak about how giving money symbolizes the giving of our lives, I just knew that I should offer my life to God in this particular way. I started to talk to my own minister, and to friends – both those who were Christians and those who weren't – and everyone seemed to think it was a great idea. The only ones who weren't too sure were my family – perhaps they knew me too well!

What were my motivations? Commitment to God? – probably. A desire to make a difference? – certainly. I had little idea of what vicars, or curates, actually did –

and any attempts I made to find out led me down an increasingly frustrating path where I got the same response from those who were already ordained of extreme busyness, but without their being able to put into words exactly what they were so busy *with*.

'What is it that you do, then, as a curate?'

The word 'curate' was originally a general term for all parish clergy – it is used in this way in the Book of Common Prayer in both its 1549 and its 1662 versions, where it means all those who share the 'cure of souls' in a particular parish. In later years, the identification of rectors and vicars as those carrying responsibility for parishes led to the associated identification of all other clergy in a parish as 'curates' – of which there were sometimes large numbers. The use of the term to mean clergy in training posts – its current meaning – emerged only fairly recently. A curacy is now, however, the starting place for almost all those who are ordained, and indicates an assistant position in a parish under the supervision of a training incumbent. The life and work that this entails will be described in more detail in subsequent chapters.

'How do *I* decide? How do *they* decide?'

The process of 'discernment' (seeking to recognize God's will) can be lengthy. The role of an ordained person is to represent the Church, and in so doing to represent God in a special, authorized way. It is a demanding job, which at times will be beyond anyone's natural abilities – but with a calling from God comes also an equipping from him. Candidates are reminded in the ordination service:

> Because you cannot bear the weight of this ministry in your own strength but only by the grace and power of God, pray earnestly for his Holy Spirit.

The testing of a call is very important, for the sake of the individual, their family and friends, the church that they will serve, and the world in which the Church exercises its ministry. It can be a frustrating process, and will demand patience and a good sense of humour! It is curiously akin to pregnancy, where there is both the desire to tell everyone what's going on, and a certain caution, especially in the early stages, arising from an uncertainty as to the possible outcome.

If the initial explorations of discernment take place in the privacy of the candidate's own heart and mind, and then with the closest circle of family and friends, the next stage sees a 'rippling out' through the local church, the local diocese and lastly the whole Church of England, through the Ministry Division. This progression enables a wider reflection upon God's calling, and for it to be seen within the wider context of God's work in the Church at a national, and not simply a local, level.

Decisions, decisions ... and dioceses

Before we go any further, a word about dioceses in the Church of England. In the organization of the Anglican Church, the primary unit is the diocese. Each diocese contains a number of parishes and is led by a bishop. The bishop 'shares' responsibility for each parish with the incumbent, usually known as the vicar or rector. (This sharing is expressed in the institution service for a new parish priest in the words: 'Receive the cure of souls for [this parish], which is both yours and mine.')

Dioceses are gathered together into provinces, and each province has its own archbishop; in England there are two provinces, Canterbury and York. Although the members of the Church in a province may come together for synods – governing bodies – to discuss important policy matters, practical matters within dioceses are under the direction of each individual bishop. This means that bishops are able to discern and act on what God is calling his Church to in each particular diocesan area – what can be called contextualization – rather than needing to follow a nationally imposed agenda. It also means, however, that there is no one single pattern for how the Church makes decisions, or carries those decisions out, across the country. For those sensing a call to ordination, this can be confusing, as one diocese's approach may vary significantly from another's.

The role of the DDO

It is your local minister who will, with your permission (reluctant or enthusiastic!), set the ball rolling, by arranging at an early stage for you to see the Diocesan Director of Ordinands (the DDO). Each diocese has a DDO who is responsible for helping anyone exploring a call to ordination to think through what it means, and whether it may be right for them. Several dioceses have more than one person sharing this responsibility, and you may find yourself meeting with a number of different people to talk about why you think God may be calling you in this way. The DDO may decide to work with you over a period of several months or even years before recommending that you attend a selection conference.

During this time, there will be opportunities for you to reflect further on your own Christian life and ministry, your understanding of ordination, and especially on your experience and understanding of the Church. A priest carries the authority of, and represents, the whole Church – not just that flavour of which they have been a part. As the Church of England is so diverse, it is important for those offering for ministry to be able, with integrity, to recognize God's work across all traditions, and to be able to work across a variety of 'churchmanships' (a way of describing the 'style' of a church's pattern of life and worship). It can come as a surprise to those who have been Christians for many years that there are many different ways of expressing faith and discipleship in the Church of England!

High church, low church, not very sure church

The Church of England has existed since the Reformation in the sixteenth century, with historical and theological roots reaching back before this through the medieval Roman Church to the original Roman and Celtic missions to this country. It has always been a diverse Church because it provides for the needs of a diverse population, identified primarily by geography rather than doctrinal position. It has also experienced successive waves of renewing movements, including the Wesleyan revivals of the eighteenth century, the evangelical and Tractarian (Anglo-Catholic, or 'high church') movements of the nineteenth century, and the liberal and charismatic movements of the twentieth century. All these have brought new life and hope to the Church, and all have left their mark – particularly on the history and contemporary life of individual parishes. Even dioceses will bear the distinctive marks of one or other of these life-bearing movements – so one diocese may have a predominantly evangelical (or 'low church') feel, whilst its neighbour may be more Catholic. The outward signs of these traditions may be in the style of clothes worn by the clergy, both 'everyday' and in the robes chosen for services. Like sacraments, these are indications of some real divergence in understanding of the nature of ministry and the Church's life. There isn't space here to describe the way in which some of these emphasize the significance of Scripture, others the tradition of God's work in the Church, others the human responsibility and solidarity that we are called to exercise, and still others the renewing contemporary work of the Spirit. A prospective minister will be ordained to represent the whole Church, and needs to be able to understand the distinctive contribution that each part brings, without which the whole would be impoverished.

The period of discerning your call in the diocese may thus include a placement in a church of a different tradition from your own. This is to give you the opportunity to discover for yourself how God may be at work in patterns of church life that you have not previously experienced – and of which you may have been quite critical.

In some dioceses, the discernment period will also include a requirement to test and develop your understanding of the role of a priest, and your reflective skills, through written assignments. As with the other parts of the process, it is unwise to view these as hoops to be jumped through, or obstacles to be negotiated with as little pain as possible. Instead, they are opportunities to think more deeply about your vocation, and to ensure that you are in tune with the Church and the Spirit as you explore the possibilities for your life.

Other pieces in the discernment jigsaw

The task of discernment is twofold: as well as seeking to establish your suitability for the ordained ministry, it also needs to build up as accurate a picture of you as possible, reflecting realistically upon your strengths and weaknesses and your particular gifts. It needs to look both to the past, and to the potential of the future, searching always for a thorough integration in your life.

Family, friends and parish

It will be important for you to take notice of the views of those who know you in as many different contexts as possible – friends, family, colleagues. You will also be asked to provide referees prior to going to a selection conference (see below) who will be able to speak about your faith, your relationships with colleagues and others, your pastoral and academic strengths, and your character. It will often be useful to sit down with your referees to help them complete the forms, which are very detailed (this information may be found on the Ministry Division website which you will find extremely useful.[1]

The support of your local parish is a vital part of the jigsaw. Some churches choose to interview candidates before adding their support to a minister's reference. Others should at the least have a discussion at the church council to reflect together on their experience of a candidate's ministry, to assist the discernment process.

Sometimes a candidate does not have the support of their local church or minister. This is not necessarily a barrier to moving on in the process, as it is recognized that there may be many reasons for a person to be looked upon in one way by a particular parish or minister whilst the wider Church would value them in a different way. Nevertheless, lack of support from a home parish or minister would of course be a cause for concern, and would need to be carefully explored.

Candidates from parishes under Alternative Episcopal Oversight – those who do not recognize or receive the ministry of ordained women priests – follow the same route for selection as other candidates. The Church of England remains committed to recognizing the diversity of beliefs about ordination, and seeks to maintain good relationships throughout the Church. The ordination of candidates from such parishes may take place in a different context from that of those from other parishes.

Divorce and remarriage

The Church of England's view on remarriage is, like many of its views, complex –
it is made up of a variety of different and sometimes contradictory attitudes held
together in what one hopes may be a godly tension. It is not, therefore, a bar to
ordination for a candidate or a candidate's spouse to have been divorced and
remarried (or to be married to a divorcee), but it is a cause for investigation. This
process is detailed, and can take some time. It will involve revisiting the history of
the breakdown of the former marriage(s), including perhaps seeking statements
from the former partner(s), with the hope of ascertaining that the present
relationship did not cause the breakdown of the earlier marriage. Attitudes to this
process will vary, and it will seem to some that matters that had been thought to
have been consigned to history will be needlessly reopened. As with other parts
of the discernment process, the candidate may choose to approach this process
with resentment or with an attitude which welcomes the opportunity to ensure
that real wounds really have been healed, and will not resurface and imperil an
otherwise valuable ministry in the future.

Medical and legal checks

Candidates are required to demonstrate that they are fit for service according
to medical and legal conditions. This will mean offering a report from their GP
(which may require a medical examination) and submitting to a Criminal Records
Bureau disclosure.

The selection conference

After the local parish and the diocese have reflected with you about the
possibility of a vocation to the ordained ministry, the decision may be taken by
your bishop, in consultation with your DDO and with your agreement, to send
you to a selection conference (Bishop's advisory panel from September 2005).
These are organized nationally by the Church of England's Ministry Division, and
are held at regular intervals in different parts of the country, usually in diocesan
retreat centres.[2] The purpose of the selection conference is to make a
recommendation to help your bishop decide whether to sponsor you for training.
It is where the national Church walks alongside the bishop in making the decision
about your vocation – but the decision remains that of the diocese (remember
that the diocese is the primary unit in the Church of England). The selectors
themselves do not make the final decision, and a bishop may overrule their
recommendation: however, if he decides to back your selection in spite of a
recommendation not to, then the bishop has an obligation to find you a training
position in his own diocese.

The Ministry Division web site describes the conference like this:

The Conference[3]

Conferences normally last from Monday to Wednesday, and you will be expected to be resident for the full time. At a conference you are likely to meet a wide range of men and women who are offering for ministry, lay or ordained. There will be a maximum of 16 candidates and a total of 6 selectors. Also present will be a Selection Secretary from the Ministry Division with whom you will already have been in touch. The selectors, drawn from all over the country, are recommended for this work by their diocesan bishops, and prepared for it by training arranged by the Ministry Division.

As the whole aim of the conference is to search out God's will for the future of the candidates, the times set aside for worship and meditation are going to be central to the whole conference programme. The rest of the time will include a personal inventory, individual interviews with selectors, a group discussion and a written exercise. All these will help the selectors to get to know you as a person and show them what stage you have reached in your understanding and experience of the Christian faith. It is hoped that you will feel free enough to open yourself to fellow candidates and selectors. This will be vital to the whole process of perceiving God's will both for you and for his Church.

In accordance with The Bishops' Criteria for Selection, selectors will want to know:

- About how you understand the tradition and practice of the Church of England.

- About your sense of vocation to ministry and mission, your own conviction and how others have confirmed it.

- About your faith and how you understand the Christian inheritance, how you seek to deepen your understanding and communicate it to others.

- About your spiritual discipline, your individual and corporate prayer and worship.

- About your maturity and stability for the demanding role of a minister; about how you face change and pressure.

- About your self-awareness and self-acceptance as a basis for developing open and healthy professional, personal and pastoral relationships. They will want to know how you will respect the will of the Church in matters of morality.

- About your ability to offer leadership in the Church community and the wider community; about your ability to offer an example of faith and discipleship and collaborate effectively with others, as well as to guide and shape the life of the Church community in its mission to the world.

- About your quality of mind and intellectual capacity to undertake satisfactorily a course of theological study and ministerial preparation and to cope with the intellectual demands of ministry.

The preparatory papers that are sent through to the selectors will prepare them to ask any necessary questions about your health or family circumstances. Although the selection is for the candidate and not their family, anyone who is selected for training who has a family will have to show that they have thought and talked through with their family the impact that training and ordination will have on their lives.

Attending a selection conference can be a daunting experience. In the past, efforts were made to 'school' candidates to know what to say to 'pass'. It is better to approach this stage of the discernment process like any other: as a chance to get to know yourself, and your place in God's purposes, better. This may mean ordination, or it may not. If it does, there is a lot of hard work ahead; if it doesn't, it is much better to find out at this stage! Those leading the conferences take pains to avoid the language of 'pass' and 'fail', and although it can still feel like this, it's worth remembering that exploring God's vocation should ultimately be a 'win – win' situation!

2

The context of ministry

Ordination is never 'on its own': to be ordained, a candidate must have a context in which they are to exercise their ministry. It could be said that this is where the two main strands of theological understanding of ordained ministry flow together: those who would stress the 'ontological' or 'being' aspects of priesthood need a place where they can 'be'; those who would stress the 'functional' or 'doing' perspective need a place where they can 'do'. There are no lone rangers in Anglican orders, roaming the land in search of challenges that they alone can resolve single-handed. Rather, each ordained ministry is rooted in a local Christian community, usually (and always in the first appointment) geographically based.

The first appointment lays the foundations from which other, more specialized ministries may develop in due course. Yet even the first appointment is not a universal foundation for all future shapes of ministry: it will fall into one of three primary categories:

- stipendiary ministry

- non-stipendiary (or 'self-supporting') ministry

- ordained local ministry.

The distinction between these is important, and may have formed the basis of the recommendation from the selection conference.

Stipendiary ministry will normally assume that the candidate is deployable anywhere in the country, whereas this may not be the case with non-stipendiary ministers and will definitely not be so for the ordained local minister, whose ministry is recognized within, and only within, the context of the local ministry team that has nurtured their vocation. As stipendiary ministry is still seen as the 'norm', we will start by revisiting this context briefly, before going on to explore the special characteristics of NSM and OLM.

Stipendiary ministry

John Witcombe

Dave and Chrissy arrived at theological college having moved only three years earlier for Dave to take up the position of youth worker in a large town centre church. They are used to moving, and to working in the goldfish bowl context of a church. They have already adjusted to the rather lower income of church work but a few years of this means that it has become increasingly difficult to replace their clothes, car, or kitchen equipment, and their resources are fairly low. Their children are preparing to move again, and anxieties about local schools, and even about adequate housing, are very pressing. They are moving to a parish within a large market town, where the church tradition will be familiar to Dave but not to Chrissy. They are looking forward to working with the incumbent, but they know that it will take them a long time to settle in another new area.

Keith and Pat were both employed in well-paid professional jobs before beginning their training. They have accepted an invitation to work in an urban context, which will mean large adjustments for them, and for their families. Their parents find it hard to understand why they have made this life decision: mixed with a grudging admiration are some large questions about the cost of the public schooling in which they invested only a few years ago. Keith and Pat are used to coping with challenges and are by nature confident people – but they find it hard to imagine what life in ministry will actually be like.

Jean was a schoolteacher before training, with a close circle of friends built up over many years in the area where she had lived for most of her life. She is returning to the same diocese, but is not sure how she is going to build her new life and maintain connections with her existing support structures. She also realizes that what she used to do for leisure – and for a sense of purpose in life – is about to become her work, and wonders what impact that will have upon her faith, as well as on her relationships.

The move into stipendiary ministry will usually involve a complete relocation of the newly ordained person, together with any family members who share their home. It will also involve change in almost every area of life. There will be a change of:

- house
- community:
  - geographical
  - church
  - employment
  - friendship/leisure
- working status
- financial provision
- rhythm of life
- personal boundaries (what was voluntary is now professional)
- relational patterns within the family
- possibly, educational provision for other family members
- ease of meeting with key supporting friends

. . . and so on. Each of these changes will bring its own bereavements, and its own hopes and challenges, but it is important to be clear that stipendiary ministry touches the whole of life.

There are many different models of living in ministry. The differences may come from church tradition, social context, or personal and domestic circumstances. Ordained ministry encompasses, and emerges from, the whole of life: it is not possible to separate work and personal life so that the one has no impact upon the other, so the shape of personal circumstances will affect the work, and vice versa. There are, however, some patterns that may usefully be identified for someone who is looking for an answer to the question, 'What do you do after you've had breakfast in the morning?'

A typical day in the life of a stipendiary curate

Prayers: often with the other members of the (ordained or otherwise recognized) ministry team, perhaps with just the vicar, or with other members of the church. May include the Eucharist. May be informal, or use the Anglican *Common Worship Daily Prayer* or *Celebrating Common Prayer*. May be at 7.00 or 9.00 a.m. – often timed around taking children to school.

In the morning:

- staff meeting: on one day of the week – perhaps for a whole morning, or over lunch
- school assembly: if there's a junior school in the parish – or, less usually, a secondary school
- Holy Communion – once midweek in most parishes
- chapter meeting: a group meeting of local Anglican clergy
- ministers' fellowship: a group meeting of local clergy from different denominations
- town centre planning group
- post-ordination training session or retreat day
- desk work: preparation for sermons, etc.
- visiting the Mums and Toddlers group

lunch at home or in a meeting.

In the afternoon, a selection of the following:

- funeral: either at the crematorium or, less often, at the church and then burial or cremation

- visits: funeral visits, hospital visits, home visiting and communions
other: service in local nursing homes or residential care complexes daytime home group;

- desk work.

Tea taken either as a break, or 'on the go' – patterns of domestic life are varied.

In the evening, one or more of the following:

- Evening Prayer or Eucharist (Evening Prayer only happens in a minority of parishes)

- Parochial Church Council (PCC) meeting

- wardens' meeting or standing committee

- other church administrative, leadership team or planning meetings

- home group/cell group or house church meeting

- monthly central fellowship meeting for prayer, Bible study or worship

- Alpha course or other evangelistic meeting

- youth group or confirmation class

- Deanery Synod (local area Anglican meeting)

- visiting – to arrange baptisms, weddings or funerals

- other visiting.

Saturdays will be quiet in some parishes, busy in others – either with weddings, or other church activities. Sunday afternoons are often quiet, and can give real space for relaxation.

It is a busy life, and boundaries are important, as we have seen. There is an inevitable loading onto the evening of activities that involve church members who are busy during the day, so it is possible, and important, to take some time out earlier on in the working day to ensure personal survival: without adequate personal resourcing, our reactions and responses will become dulled, and possibly quite damaging to those around us. The parishioner who has come to a meeting from a busy day at work or caring for the family when they would rather crash on the settee in front of the TV at home may not have much sympathy for the reluctant curate, who sees this meeting as her work but the parishioner's leisure. It can be useful to think of the day as made up of three or four parts — morning, afternoon, early evening, late evening, for example — and commit to taking one of these parts as leisure time, for personal refreshment and resourcing. No one runs well on empty, and neither vocation to servant ministry nor the special anointing of ordination gives the minister exemption from the need for rest and recovery. Ways of doing this are explored in Chapter 7.

Non-stipendiary ministry

Margaret Whipp

It is surprising how little is generally known about the non-stipendiary mode of ministry, which I have come to appreciate as one of the Church of England's best-kept secrets. Yet non-stipendiary ministers account for nearly 20 per cent of the clergy in England, and this proportion is steadily rising.

Why 'non-stipendiary'? At first glance it's an odd label to attach to anyone's vocation. This section will explore some of the rich diversity of ministries that are being developed by non-stipendiaries. If you have always thought that full-time stipendiary ministry is the only 'proper' way of serving the Church, then this section will help you to think outside the box about some of the more flexible ways of fulfilling a priestly vocation. If you are already moving towards non-stipendiary ministry, then you will appreciate the importance of defining and developing a ministry that is of enormous worth, for God and his kingdom.

What's in a name?

NSM, APM, MSE, SSM – the Church has struggled to find an adequate name for a form of ministry that can be gloriously diverse and unpredictable. For administrative purposes the usual term is non-stipendiary ministry (NSM), although, as we shall see, there is a lot more to be said about this model of ministry than that the Church doesn't have to pay for it!

Most people are not embarrassed by the negative connotation in the label 'NSM'. They are glad to be in a position to offer their time and skills as a gift to the Christian community. Some, however, are sensitive to the inevitable prejudice of a money-oriented society which fails to value what it does not pay for. They appreciate the more positive emphasis in the label 'self-supporting ministry' (SSM), which affirms the worthwhileness of unpaid service, although arguably it draws undue attention to the financial security and largesse of the minister. An older unhelpful term, 'auxiliary pastoral ministry' (APM), has now been dropped. National experience of non-stipendiary ministry confirms that there are many highly able people who exercise ministries of considerable responsibility in both church and community, often with a distinctively prophetic rather than a solely pastoral vision. Some now prefer the designation 'minister in secular employment' (MSE). This term is mainly used to underline the significance of their presence in the world of work.

Being categorized

The Church's process of discernment necessarily takes place within a wider context of financial planning for future ministry. For this reason it is usual to specify in advance a 'category' within which a candidate for ministry will be recommended for training. Yet such advance specification leaves little room for a continuing exploration of vocation that may lead in unexpected directions. Alongside the traditional categories of stipendiary, (permanent) non-stipendiary and ordained local ministry, there is also a fluid category of 'stipendiary/non-stipendiary ministry' which is now applied more frequently by the dioceses so as to leave a wider range of options open for the future.

'Nobody likes to be defined by a negative ...' A workshop for NSMs in training explored how their future role might be perceived. NSMs are not paid, not appreciated, not taken seriously, not respected as professionals, some suggested. But others were excited by the ways in which NSMs are not tied to outmoded models of ministry, not boxed in by other people's expectations, not limited in the scope of their mission, not restricted to conventional roles in the Church. They have a share in the radical pattern of Jesus' ministry, which resisted any conventional categorization:

- Jesus resisted the label 'Teacher' (Mark 10.17-18);

- Jesus refused to be designated a 'Judge' (Luke 12.13-14);

- Jesus rejected the title of 'Rabbi' or 'Father' and subverted conventional models of authority (Matthew 23.1-12 and 21.23-7).

'Nobody likes to be defined by a negative' – but it leaves much more scope for the imagination!

Are you focused?

There is no single model for non-stipendiary ministry. Much will depend on the home circumstances and/or the employment responsibilities of the individual. An important question to consider from the time of discernment and throughout training is how the focus of your future ministry will be identified. A *parish-focused NSM* sees the context of ministry in much the same way as his stipendiary colleagues; a *work-focused NSM* sees the sphere of her ministry predominantly in terms of her workplace and wider professional networks.

John is a retired teacher with long-standing links in the local community. He is a parish-focused NSM who has developed a valuable outreach to families. He also has pastoral charge of one of the villages within the benefice.

Paul is a solicitor working in a busy practice supporting many clients through legal aid. He is a work-focused NSM who extends pastoral care to many people who would never approach the church. He is also politically active within his profession, addressing issues of social justice at a national level.

Jackie is a former administrator, and mother of a young family. She is a parish-focused NSM who offers important additional skills to the parish ministry team whilst also developing her ministry within the diocese as a spiritual director.

Penny is the director of an early learning centre. She works with deprived families and coordinates care between a variety of statutory and voluntary bodies. She is a work-focused NSM who has discovered a growing ministry as informal spiritual guide to parents with no links to the church. She also recognizes that she performs a ministry to the structures of education and social services, being used as a significant resource in developing their understanding of spirituality.

> Maria works part-time in the community advice centre. She is
> able to give considerable time to parish ministry as well as to her
> paid work. She values both the parish focus and the work focus,
> and is appreciated for her bridge-building role in bringing together
> church people and others around common community concerns.

Being deployed

The Church has no single strategy for the deployment of NSMs. Some candidates
offer for this form of ministry assuming that they will remain in their own
congregation and parish, rather like an OLM. This is not necessarily a good thing,
either for the candidate or for the mission of the wider Church. Many dioceses
now make a distinction between NSMs, who are selected and trained for a
ministry that could take them anywhere in the country, and OLMs, who are
selected and trained with the needs of a specific parish ministry team in view.
Although an NSM will usually have his own home and be tied to an area by
family or business commitments, it is now more common for an NSM to be
licensed to a parish different from his home church, at least in the early stages
of gaining experience in ministry.

So you're a part-timer?

This question may be raised in a half-joking way, but behind it lies a profoundly
serious issue. Can a priest ever be part-time? Are there any times when she is
anything other than a minister of the gospel?

The spirituality of the NSM is a spirituality of the whole of life. Not only her
'churchy' activities but also her everyday involvement in the community of the
workplace or the neighbourhood become part of her ministry. She is a sign
of God's presence wherever she lives and moves and has her being.

Being a priest in the world of work

The Church in Wales identified a number of roles that the NSM might fulfil in the
course of a normal working day:

- an *interpreter* of the Church to the world, and of the world to the Church;
- an informal *teacher* in down-to-earth theology and ethics;
- a *counsellor* with an understanding of problems born of shared experience;
- a *confessor*, speaking wisely of repentance and forgiveness;
- a *comforter* to the distressed and bereaved;

- a *mediator* between men and women and God and between different people, whether as individuals or groups;

- an *intercessor* who prays for all with whom and for whom she works;

- the *nucleus* for Christian groups.

The NSM is an important boundary figure, placed on the frontier between the Church and what is sometimes called the secular world. From this perspective, she can discern God's activity in some surprising places. She asks the question, 'What does God look like if you don't start in church?', and finds some very interesting answers. Because she is at home in the secular environment, she can speak with a natural voice, and share the journey of faith with others whose starting point may be far removed from the Church.

Of course, she needs to respect important boundaries, to protect herself and others from unreasonable intrusion. Taking time off work on a regular basis to help with parish funerals, for example, is not likely to impress working colleagues! Yet within the trusting relationships that develop among close colleagues, where pastoral care is shared over the coffee machine rather than across the communion rail, the NSM is an accessible focus of God's loving presence.

Being identified

Most work-focused NSMs choose not to wear a dog collar at work. It could be quite intimidating, for example, in the relationship between a teacher and his pupils, or a doctor and her patients. What matters is an openness, and an appropriate sensitivity about sharing the representative role.

Yvonne is the manager of a small bakery. She does not claim to run a 'Christian' shop, but customers and colleagues know that they can ask for 'prayer with their pastries' when times are hard.

Peter is a hospital physiotherapist. The title 'Reverend' is shown on his name badge. He waits for patients to ask him, 'Are you going to minister to my soul as well as my body?'

John works in marketing. His boss was initially worried that ordination might blunt his competitive edge. Nine months later, he is realizing that customers are curious to know more about the 'company curate'. He has asked John to put the title 'Reverend' on his business cards.

Looking ahead

About 200 men and women are being ordained for non-stipendiary ministry each year. What will the future hold for them? Should they expect to 'serve a title' in the same way as a stipendiary curate? Will they be most fruitfully deployed in the same parish for their entire ministry? Or should they envisage an imaginative development of their apostolic ministry that may be less predictable than the default model of parish ministry anticipated by their stipendiary colleagues?

NSMs can be a rich resource for a Church that is learning new ways of reaching out to a changing society. Yet many NSMs encounter a lack of imagination in the Church when it comes to deploying and developing their non-traditional role. I have found that a good spiritual director or work consultant can be an invaluable help in discerning the potential of a ministry that might otherwise be underdeveloped.

What are you training for?

Stipendiary curates can be relatively clear about their training needs. All of them will need help to reflect on the realities of parish ministry in practice, and most of them will go on to posts of responsibility as an incumbent.

The learning needs of non-stipendiary curates are less uniform and predictable. Some of them may be preparing for an incumbent-style parish ministry or a permanent associate ministry, whilst others will be exploring models of ministry in secular employment or other specialist roles on the edge of the parish structure.

- What sort of training incumbent will be most helpful to a work-focused NSM? (It may not be the vicar who complained that MSE meant 'mostly somewhere else'!)

- How much of the traditional diet of CME (or post-ordination training) will be relevant or accessible to an NSM who is in full-time secular work?

- What other structures might be helpful in exploring non-traditional patterns of ministry (work consultant, diocesan support group, CHRISM network[1])?

A day in the life of a non-stipendiary curate

Patrick gets up at 6.45 a.m. to the strains of the local radio. Largely on autopilot, he makes the cup of tea that will help him gather his thoughts for morning prayer. Today's reading is from Philippians 4: 'Whatever is true, whatever is honourable ... think on these things.' It's the text on a poster he has displayed in his classroom at school. Family breakfast over, he has a few minutes' time to collect his thoughts on the way to school. So many of the staff are under pressure because of an impending restructure that it's hard to keep focused on the needs of the children. He finds he is quietly praying for those he will work with today.

The second lesson is disrupted by a pupil who is sniggering at some secret magazine. It turns out to be a foul racist publication. Patrick deals with the challenge by starting a discussion about values. One of the other children quotes the poster on the wall: 'Whatever is true, whatever is honourable ...' Racism is degrading. Everyone deserves respect. The ethos of the classroom is gently restored. Silently, Patrick thanks God.

Lunch is shared with a colleague who is buckling under career pressures. There's nothing much to be said; after all, the staff are all in the same stressful boat. But Patrick is known as someone who will listen and, perhaps, also as someone who will quietly pray.

The evening is spent at home catching up with family issues. Patrick shares the bed-time duties with his wife, then settles down for an hour's reading. He is preparing a presentation for next week's PCC meeting, but gets waylaid when a house group leader phones to talk through his anxieties about some destructive behaviour in the meeting. Carving out time for study and preparation is almost harder for a non-stipendiary curate than for a full-timer, and Patrick tries not to feel resentful when precious time is spent on the phone.

At the end of a long day, the text from Philippians is still permeating Patrick's thoughts. Priorities may be hard to establish, but for a Christian minister some values are non-negotiable. 'Whatever is true, whatever is honourable ...' Patrick goes to bed thinking on these things.

Being used and being valued

Ordained ministry is a precious gift, yet it is a gift that can be wasted or squandered if it is not properly used and valued. Non-stipendiary ministry is particularly precious because it carries a degree of freedom that is impossible in stipendiary ministry. Precisely because of its ambiguous position, it is a gift that must be carefully protected from misuse or lack of respect.

Some NSMs are underused and undervalued. Their spiritual gifts and wider talents are seen as a threat to stipendiary clergy, so they are marginalized. Their ministry is not encouraged or developed, so it becomes a source of frustration.

Some NSMs are overused and undervalued. Their willingness to serve is exploited, and their time and talents are not properly respected. They are used as willing horses, their ministry is taken for granted, so they become weary and resentful.

Occasionally NSMs are overvalued yet underused. They are treated as a rare commodity, combining unusual skills and perspectives for which neither they nor anyone else in the church can find a fruitful outlet. With their talents largely unharnessed, they turn into eccentrics and dilettantes.

The ideal situation is achieved only through prayerful negotiation and the honest support of advisers and colleagues. The NSM, whether work-focused or parish-focused, is wisely used and warmly valued. Her gifts are encouraged, her vision of ministry is nurtured and developed, and she can trust that in some specific way her work and her whole life are serving the kingdom of God.

Ordained local ministry

Eileen Turner

> Tracey and Clive both live in the Potteries.[2] Tracey is in her 30s and has two teenage children still at home. She works part-time in a gym and on Saturday nights you can find her behind the bar of the local pub. The decision to become a barmaid was taken at the time she was ordained. The thought of ordination never entered her head until her church suggested she might become their ordained local minister.[3]

> Clive is a chartered accountant in his 50s. As a young man he
> was bitterly disappointed when he was not recommended for
> ordination training. More recently he has found enormous
> satisfaction ministering alongside others in a local leadership
> team, realizing that he was never suited to the 'one-man-band'
> traditional model. He runs his own business and can afford to
> be semi-retired, releasing more time to serve as an OLM.

Both Tracey and Clive trained on the Local Ministry Scheme in Lichfield Diocese. Their ministries are focused in the local church, but in effect are much wider than that. Each has lived their whole life in the locality and can identify with the community in a way that their fellow clergy rarely do. The 'visible' sign of ordination not only enhances that role – hence Tracey's 'Saturday-night-and-Sunday-morning' stint in pub–church – but curiously gives confidence to the whole community as it sees 'one of its own' holding a role previously associated with the 'professional' incomer.

Complementary forms of ministry

> Alan is a college-trained curate. At his ordination retreat he
> found himself alongside Maureen, an early-retired woman who
> turned out to be his new OLM colleague. He was shocked to
> discover that, in spite of what he privately thought of as her
> 'second-class' training, she was immediately given some
> responsibilities he had been led to believe 'belonged' in the
> second year of a curacy! Even worse (though he never
> articulated this), Maureen lived in a nicer house, 'had the ear'
> of many of the congregation and reminded him of his mum![4]

Alan's training had been more high-powered academically and had majored on many areas essential for his future role as an incumbent. For Maureen, the integrated approach to formation on an OLM scheme had given a fuller preparation for some pastoral aspects of the job. Alan's ordination signalled sudden change in almost every aspect of life. For Maureen, and for the church, ordination was an important public marker of an almost imperceptible process. His first year included the hard graft of familiarizing himself with a new community plus energetic tasks like organizing a youth group and experimenting with new forms of worship. During that same year she built on her existing knowledge of the parish, training a team to visit nursing homes and sheltered accommodation, and sharing weddings and marriage preparation with the vicar. Alan had to acknowledge his competitiveness not only with respect to Maureen but also to the other members of the local leadership team, who were used to having a large say in decision-making.

If, like Clive or Tracey or Maureen, you have been ordained as a local minister, you will discover it an exciting, fulfilling, and probably a far more demanding way of life than you ever anticipated. If, like Alan, you are inclined to be suspicious, or have never heard of OLM, I hope this chapter will bring enlightenment.

Local ministry teams

Given the relative youthfulness of this expression of priesthood, it is worth taking a more detailed look at its context and history. Ordained local ministers are relative newcomers to the Church of England, though their numbers are increasing rapidly. Since the mid-1980s, when the first scheme was established, almost half our dioceses have joined in and there are currently 447 OLMs spread over 20 dioceses.[6] The collaborative teams, a prerequisite for OLM, vary enormously. In a small village near Keele, OLM Sally is the only ordained team member. Her main task of sacramental ministry and pastoral care is supported by several others who share the traditional 'vicar' role, and she operates under the oversight of a stipendiary in the next village. In urban Wolverhampton, two OLMs are part of the team ministry that covers several 'parishes' by means of a complex but successful structure of interlinked teams including lay and clergy, paid and unpaid, full-time and part-time.

At the heart of OLM is the idea of Local Ministry, the 'ministry of all the baptized'.[6] Diocesan schemes are much more than training courses. Most offer a consultation process to help parishes develop ministry patterns appropriate for their context and, when certain criteria are satisfied, these are often 'mandated' by the bishop.[7] Best practice includes wide consultation with the church and the community, often involving a 'calling out process' for all team members. The idea of the local church 'inviting' a candidate to consider ordination is unusual in Anglican tradition, though it may well be the best place to recognize a call.[8] OLM training varies considerably in shape, usually including components for the local team but also overlapping with diocesan lay training or regional courses.[9]

This is still a non-starter in some dioceses. One major objection is that OLMs are 'non-deployable priests', which is often seen as a contradiction in terms. Another argument, perhaps more persuasive but less often articulated, is that the collaborative nature of OLM subverts the hierarchical structure that still prevails in the Church of England. It is more radical than simply encouraging lay leadership.[10] Local ministry is about the whole *laos* participating in God's work both inside and outside the Church.[11] In other parts of the Anglican Communion it is known as 'Total Ministry' or 'Mutual Ministry' — the Church is seen as 'a ministering community' rather than 'a community gathered round its minister'. This 'new way of being church' is characterized by openness, flexibility, transparency, trust and risk.[12] I am convinced that this is consistent with biblical patterns of ministry, is bringing a fresh injection of energy into the Church, and may turn out to be a major factor in helping the Church of England in the essential task of reinventing itself. But it can seem new and painful for those who do not like change.

Earlier influences

But these ideas are not really new. John Tiller talked this 'language' 20 years ago, though at first he was largely ignored.[13] Good practice often goes ahead of theory, and many churches that were experimenting with new styles of ministry began to ask for official recognition. Two working party reports in the 1990s rapidly filled in the background thinking, stressing the need to encourage 'indigenous' ministries, the growth of collaborative teams which included both lay and ordained people, and the idea that a 'local' priesthood is certainly not 'second class'. They noted the need to complement the work of decreasing numbers of stipendiaries but stressed that this must never be the driving force. The second report, *Stranger in the Wings,* emphasized how much hard work is needed to develop collaborative, as distinct from delegated, ministry.[14] OLMs were never expected to be simply 'mass priests', filling in for overstretched incumbents. Some do find themselves working outside the collaborative context, perhaps persuaded by someone in authority to take on a quasi-vicar role to keep open a failing church, but then their distinctiveness disappears.[15]

Roland Allen, a missionary in China in the last century who is often hailed as another 'prophet before his time', believed that early church leaders were appointed in groups, with built-in mechanisms for replacement so that authority was always shared. He was convinced that this pattern of corporate leadership can be recreated and that the inclusion of 'local priests' is essential for a healthy church.[16] It is certainly arguable that what became known as 'presbyteral' ministry in the early Church was not simply about individuals embodying every aspect of leadership, but was a corporate description of publicly authorized ministry, appropriate today for local lay leaders as well as local or stipendiary priests.[17] This is true of many Anglican provinces where a team of voluntary local ministers (lay and ordained) are supported by a small number of salaried clergy.[18] The Church of England may well be moving towards such a pattern.[19]

Priestly identity

The idea of 'priesthood' is also crucial to our understanding of OLM.[20] The priestly role of mediation between God and the world has been taken on by Jesus, who calls the whole Church to make real what he has done.[21] But we still need a 'ministerial priesthood' to facilitate this.[22] Vincent Donovan, who worked among the Masai people in the 1960s, believed that new cultural situations would produce less individualistic forms of priesthood than we have seen in the past.[23] He noticed that each tribe included someone who could draw people together – not necessarily the most intelligent, or the best teacher, or the one who took initiatives, but the person who enabled others to act both individually and together. Later, after some Masai had become Christians, he asked what local term was equivalent to 'priest'. Rejecting many 'leadership' words, they suggested one which meant 'helper' – the only person who could bring a community into existence and enable it to function.[24] The Diocese of Nevada uses the phrase 'gatherer of the community' to describe this quality, the priest's distinctive contribution in helping the Church discover its meaning.[25] I have noticed that this gift is most effective when it is identified in someone who truly belongs to a community: people like Tracey, for example, who, because of their educational or social background, might previously have been overlooked. This quality of 'focusing' the ministry of others may well be the essence of priesthood and is totally consistent with the New Testament picture of the Church as the Body of Christ requiring a multitude of interdependent ministries.

OLM today

So OLM opens up a route into priesthood for a wider spectrum of people – but it is not a 'back door' route into ordination and it is certainly not 'second class'.[26] If you feel you are being called in this direction you will face more hurdles than other candidates, for in addition to the normal selection procedure, there will be extensive consultation at parish level. Thankfully, you do not have to pretend to be a 'jack of all trades', but the 'essential gift' described above can only be discerned by others. Training is rigorous and includes elements for the leadership team as well as the individual. If you have been a Reader, used to a peripatetic preaching ministry, you may find your wings are clipped as the focus of OLM ministry narrows.[27] You may also have to face the fear of being trapped, unable to move churches or contemplate transfer to another category of ministry.[28] The whole thing is a non-starter if your diocese does not encourage OLM: though you could begin lobbying, and in the meantime foster genuine collaborative ministry so that your church is ready to leap into action as soon as policy is changed!

After ordination you will find yourself facing a whole range of reactions. Although most OLMs hold their own in clergy circles, there will be some painful exceptions. You will share the experience of many women who, ten years after their ordination as priests, still find themselves answering naïve questions about their role! To many in your community you will be indistinguishable from other clergy (everyone knows that anyone in a cassock is a vicar!). You will almost certainly have many ministerial opportunities that are denied to deployable clergy, but this may cause tension with colleagues. At the same time, the very nature of the role means that sometimes you 'cannot see the wood for the trees', so you will be reliant on the stimulation and new insights of 'itinerant' colleagues. Hardest of all, you will discover that it is no easy option to be a 'representative person' in a community where you are known 'warts and all'. You cannot move on after your 'curacy' and leave your mistakes behind! A high level of maturity and personal integrity is required in what I believe is the most demanding form of priestly ministry.

A typical week in the life of an OLM?

OLMs are encouraged to have some form of written agreement, though there are probably as many job descriptions as there are OLMs! For someone with a demanding day job, the commitment might be a stint on Sunday and one other evening, plus preparation time. At the other end of the spectrum, many who can afford to be financially self-supporting become involved with the whole round of visiting, occasional offices, school assemblies, committees and so on! The danger of becoming a workaholic is as great as for stipendiary colleagues, and help is needed to keep the discipline of regular days off. Others have particular responsibilities appropriate to their gifting, such as heading up a healing and prayer ministry or developing new ways of being church. For some, like Robert, a community worker in Burton-upon-Trent, the main sphere of ministry is in the world outside the Church. Since ordination, he has found his 'day job' developing in unexpected ways and now it has become almost impossible to distinguish between his role as a community worker and his priestly task. Whatever their working pattern, all OLMs are conscious that their ministry is rooted in the worship of the local church, and many make a great effort to say the office with other team members when they can, even if this is not possible every day.

Hope for the future

The Church of England is experimenting with new ideas. Many of these are innovative, appealing to the young and mobile, but reinforce traditional ministry styles. Churches that really encourage every-member ministry are not always the fastest growing, nor do they have the highest profile, but their confidence in rediscovering the variety of ministry typical of the early Church may offer the best chance of long-term growth. Often OLMs play a significant part in that as well as relieving the problem of fewer stipendiary clergy. But if you are a 'career incumbent', all this represents a huge challenge. You will need specialist skills, your role may change many times during your working life, and you will need simultaneously to manage both traditional and new patterns of church life.[29]

Imagine that we revisit Tracey, Clive and the others a dozen years down the line. Tracey's parish has been subject to 'pastoral reorganization' in a big way, though the core of the original leadership team survives and Tracey still boasts that she has never spent more than one week at a time outside the parish. Due to unexpected family circumstances Clive found himself moving to a diocese that did not have OLM. After many interviews and a little further training he is now an NSM, provided with accommodation in the parish in which he works. Maureen struggles with ill health but still manages to give three days a week to her parish. After a long vacancy, when the leadership team really proved its worth, came a rocky period when she and her new incumbent found each other very threatening. But they survived intact and the church moved into a new phase with even more members mobilized to do God's work, both in the church and in their daily lives. Alan, still young and energetic, is in his third post, relying on his considerable gifts, skills and experience as he organizes a large group of parishes. His painful time as a curate in a local leadership team has reaped great benefits, for he can sit loose to the 'power trip' experienced by many incumbents and happily live with the risky business of encouraging all Christians to exercise their previously undiscovered gifts.

For further reading

Non-stipendiary ministry

James M. M. Francis and Leslie J. Francis (eds), *Tentmaking: Perspectives on Self-Supporting Ministry*, Gracewing, 1998.

Rod Hacking, *On the Boundary: A Vision for Non-Stipendiary Ministry*, Canterbury Press, 1990.

Michael Ranken, *How God Looks If You Don't Start in Church*, Cairns Publications, 2001.

Report to the Bench of Bishops of the Working Group on the Self-Supporting Ministry, Church in Wales Publications, 1981.

Ordained local ministry

Roland Allen, *Missionary Methods St Paul's or Ours?*, Lutterworth Press, 1968.

Christopher Cocksworth and Rosaline Brown, *Being a Priest Today: Exploring Priestly Identity*, Canterbury Press, 2002.

Steven Croft, *Ministry in Three Dimensions*, Darton, Longman & Todd, 1999.

Robin Greenwood, *Transforming Priesthood*, SPCK, 1994.

Robin Greenwood, *Practising Community: The Task of the Local Church*, SPCK, 1996.

Robin Greenwood, *The Ministry Team Handbook*, SPCK, 2000.

George Guiver et al., *The Fire and the Clay*, SPCK, 1993.

George Guiver et al., *Priests in a People's Church*, SPCK, 2002.

Gerard Kelly, *Get a Grip on the Future*, Monarch Books, 1999.

A. M. Ramsey, *The Christian Priest Today*, SPCK, 1972.

Alastair Redfern, *Ministry and Priesthood*, Darton, Longman & Todd, 1999.

Stewart C. Zabriskie, *Total Ministry*, Alban Institute, 1997.

3

Getting started: training and finding a curacy

John Witcombe

Once the selection conference is over, there is usually a wait of up to two weeks before you hear the outcome of the bishop's decision, based on the selectors' report. The report is just over two pages long and includes a paragraph from each of the selectors, reflecting their conversations with you and their observations of you during the conference together with the paperwork they have received prior to the conference. It is now open to your examination (under the Data Protection Act) and will often offer a concise yet profound insight into your Christian life. It will conclude with one of three possible recommendations: 'Recommended for training', 'Conditionally recommended for training' or 'Not recommended for training'.

Recommended for training

If you are offering for stipendiary or non-stipendiary ministry, this will mean training either at a theological *college* or on one of the regional, non-residential theological *courses*. If you are offering for ordained local ministry (OLM), it will mean training on a diocesan OLM *scheme*. Your training is likely to begin the following September. The Church of England is currently reviewing its arrangements for training, looking especially at establishing Regional Training Partnerships: it is not yet clear what the impact of these will be on the choices available to candidates.

Conditionally recommended for training

The selectors will sometimes observe a need for further development before recognized training can usefully begin. This may be in the area of personal, academic or spiritual development, and will be explored with you by your DDO.

Not recommended for training

It's always hard not to be chosen for something – even if that something isn't right for us! Your DDO or bishop will help you think through what other options are right for you, if the conference does not discern a place for you in ordained ministry.

Each of the three possible outcomes relates to *training*, not to *ordination*. The recommendation of the selection conference relates only to the next stage of the journey, and does not in itself – even for a recommended candidate – guarantee that the Church will ordain that person. This decision is made as training progresses, and is subject not only to satisfactory progress being made, but also to the successful identification of the right parish context for the candidate to begin their ordained ministry.

Training routes

Those training for ordained local ministry will all train on a scheme operating in their area. For others, the decision about which training route to follow is, like many other aspects of training, made jointly by the candidate and their diocese. At present, around half train in a theological college and half on a part-time course. A small but increasing number combine these forms in a 'mixed-mode' scheme, with periods of residence combined with first lay and then ordained ministry.[1] At the heart of any training is ministerial formation.

Training in a theological college offers a complete break from former life for both the candidate and their family, coupled with immersion into a community that is wholly dedicated to preparation for ministry. This can be a wonderful opportunity to reflect in the company of others and to devote all your attention to the necessary disciplines of spirituality, theology and personal development. Financial constraints are now making this training route more difficult for some, but it remains a unique environment for the transitions which formation requires.

Part-time training offers the chance to maintain existing networks of friendships, which can be especially valuable for candidates with families. Community is an equally important part of this form of training, although it is a 'part-time' community, coming together for training evenings and weekends, and summer or Easter schools.

A third option for some candidates is to commute weekly to a residential centre of training. This can work very well for those who would like the sense of immersion that theological college training gives, but who need to maintain an existing domestic base, often for family reasons. It is usually possible to arrange placements local to the area in which a student lives, so that they are only away from home from Monday to Friday, allowing them to concentrate on college work whilst at college, and on the family whilst at home, which can offer the best of both worlds.

At present, candidates under 30 will normally be required to train at theological college for three years (unless they hold a theology degree, which may exempt them from a year's study). Those between the ages of 30 and 50 will train for either two years at theological college (stipendiary candidates only), or for three years on a part-time course. Those aged 50 or above may well train for a shorter period at their bishop's discretion. The difference in the length of training can be justified on the basis of the life and Christian experience of older candidates. It also makes good sense on both financial and motivational grounds: no one will want to spend a great proportion of their remaining working life in training!

Candidates for non-stipendiary ministry will normally, but not necessarily, be offered a three-year training programme on a regional course. There are twelve ministerial training courses in the country, each designed with the local geography and the pastoral needs of the dioceses they serve in mind. Some courses have a centralized, urban ethos, others have a more dispersed mode of operation appropriate to relatively rural regions.

Now that so much initial ministerial education takes place on regional courses, some of the outdated prejudices about this form of training are being challenged. It is not a soft option, nor is it an academically lightweight alternative to the traditional college experience. Students on courses are selected by the same criteria, and their educational programmes are validated by both the Church and the local university according to the same rigorous expectations as are applied to theological colleges. It is important, however, to appreciate the differences in learning experience between a course that is undertaken in the midst of continuing responsibilities in everyday life, and a college programme that is pursued as a full-time commitment for a shorter period of time:

- The great strength of a regional course is the opportunity it provides for contextual learning. With no disconnection from the ongoing relationships and responsibilities of daily life, there is a real impetus to relate theological and pastoral studies to the realities of everyday life. A project that may be explored at the weekend in relation to biblical concepts of justice is immediately brought face to face with the ethical realities of work on Monday morning.

- An exciting challenge on a regional course is the diverse learning community. Unlike colleges, which historically serve the particular needs of different traditions within the Church, the regional courses have a greater balance of candidates, from whatever background or churchmanship. Many courses are ecumenical, including Methodist and URC ministers in training, and some also involve lay students. A student from a deep-rooted tradition in one wing of the Church will develop firm friendships with people from contrasting backgrounds, and enlarge their spiritual understanding and theological sympathies as a result.

• One of the great assets of the regional courses is their network of local resource people. Students who train within their own region will engage with a host of local advisors, tutors, supervisors and mentors, all of whom will continue to be available for friendship and support in the early days of ministry.

• Time management is an essential discipline for anyone undertaking this kind of training. A typical course will demand between 12 and 15 hours per week. Some students are able to give more time; others have to negotiate blocks of time which they can devote to study over a concentrated period. Learning how to set personal priorities and establish sustainable rhythms for the working week and the working year are vitally important skills for future ministry!

Each training route makes huge demands on candidates, and none is an easy option. Even those training on a part-time basis will find that they have to give up their existing church or community responsibilities to fulfil the demands of the course. Those who train at theological college, but in their own area, may find this an especially difficult challenge. Much has been said about the 'de-skilling' of those in ordination training, as they leave their positions of responsibility (and identity) in church and employment. This can expose serious areas of weakness in a person's self-identity, which can then be helpfully addressed. Equally, it can appear to devalue a person's former ministry, and this is to be strenuously resisted.

Whatever form of training is undertaken, it will address the following areas:

• Character – *the mirror*. Candidates learn to look closely at themselves in a mirror, recognizing the impact that their own history and personality will have on their ministry. Community provides an invaluable tool in this task of self-awareness, as we most often recognize (and react against) the weaknesses in others that are actually our own. The acceptance of diversity in a community will lead to a healthy acceptance of the diversity within ourselves. Failure to embrace this diversity will become apparent in a community context, and may suggest the need for some personal development prior to ordination.

• Analytical skills – *the trowel and the magnifying glass*. It is important for candidates to learn to dig below the surface of an issue: to move beyond the question 'What's going on?' to the more profound 'What's *really* going on?' This will demand a knowledge of a wide range of diagnostic tools, and a willingness to ask hard questions. Those who are ordained need to look beyond superficial answers, which tend to stereotype the world, to understand the complexity of personal and social relationships – before seeking to discern the hand of God in their midst. They need to be able to see the world through the eyes of others, to avoid giving theological justification to their own prejudices, and to equip themselves to become partners in the work for justice and reconciliation.

- Theological skills – *the map or guide book and the compass*. Many students come to a college or a course seeking theological understanding, and they are richly rewarded. To learn theology is to learn to discern the ways of God's interaction with his people and his world, to learn to be partners in the building of the kingdom. Paul Ballard and John Pritchard, in their useful book Practical Theology in Action, offer these four functions for theology:

  - It is *descriptive* – it enables us to give name and order to our experience.

  - It is *normative* – it enables us to test our experience and reflection against that which has been identified as representing authentic Christian tradition.

  - It is *critical* – it enables us to ask questions of our own tradition, to develop it and deepen it.

  - It is *apologetic* – it enables us to present our faith to those who do not share it.[2]

  Without theology we are simply creating our own best ideas of how to be and what to work for. Theology is a demanding discipline, in which the answers may appear more elusive the more one searches, but it is an indispensable tool for the ministers of the Church.

- Professional ministerial skills – *the Black & Decker*. It may seem that training for ministry should be primarily about the practicalities of the job – how to get up the steps of a pulpit without tripping over your cassock, or how to celebrate communion. It must include these things (although many of them will be learnt more effectively 'on the job' than in the simulated environment of a college or course) – but it must not start with them! To begin with the exercise of ministry, rather than with the formation of the character of the minister, would be to court disaster for the future. To exercise authorized ministry is to have a powerful tool placed in one's hands – just like a power tool from the local DIY store. It is possible to wield such a tool to great effect, either positive or negative, and proper training needs to be given!

Training for ministry is adult and collaborative. In common with the earlier stages in the discernment process, it is important to overcome a sense of 'jumping through hoops': the training is for a purpose, not simply a means to an end. Areas of weakness that emerge in training should be explored and addressed with the help of tutors – this is the purpose of the preparation. It is common for candidates to receive support with both personal and academic issues, perhaps through a course of counselling or personal tutorial support. To receive such support willingly is a sign of strength, not weakness.

Vocation to the training community

When you are exploring ordination it's natural to be looking ahead to your future ministry when you are considering where your vocation lies. However, it's well worth considering your vocation at each stage of the process of preparation, and this includes the part you will play – both contributing to as well as receiving from – in the community of formation. Training institutions, whether colleges or courses, are only as rich as the current membership: they rely on students as well as staff putting in all they can. You are not to be simply a passive recipient of knowledge or information.

A training institution is a strange creature. It's sometimes said that it's 'not the real world'. This is of course true to an extent – it's a hothouse, an artificial environment. Yet, if the 'real world' is characterized by relationships and growth in personal and social life, then theological courses and colleges are like a 'super-concentrated' part of the real world. They are to be lived through in the richest way possible. Rather like airport departure lounges, they are full of strange and unusual diversions, and you only enter them because you're on your way to somewhere else. Some people, though, are able to make even this stage a part of the holiday, or journey, on which they are embarking, and it becomes important in the establishing of relationships prior to take-off, providing opportunities for both reflection and anticipation – as well as necessary last-minute preparation!

Training and formation

The purpose of training is 'formation'. As the Ministry Division puts it:

> The purpose of your training is to equip you for a ministry in which you are continually learning and growing. Developing a more thorough knowledge of the Christian faith – in the scriptures and through the life, worship and teaching of the Church – is an important part of that purpose. But alongside the development of your thinking must go growth in faith and disciplined, personal communion with God; the acquiring of

ministerial skills and an understanding of the world around us; and a growing awareness of the sort of person you are and how you relate to others. Training itself is and ought to be a demanding experience. It is part of continuing to discern your vocation and seeing what sort of ministry is appropriate for you.[3]

Your training is not finished when you leave the college or course. It continues throughout your life: one of the primary purposes of training is to give you the tools to become a lifelong learner, someone who continually reflects upon their experience of life, and ministry, and who grows in maturity and wisdom.

Formation is the process of becoming a person who can stand for the Church as the Church stands for Christ in the world. It means learning to stand, laugh, cry and walk with others as Christ does. It means learning to lead others into God's presence in worship and prayer, and so much more. It means taking in the life-blood, the spirituality of the Church, so that it runs naturally in you. It is only possible to exercise this ministry in collaboration with others, so it means learning who you are in the context of the Church's community, and in the context of your own particular gifts and calling.

The academic side of training: degrees and diplomas

As a part of your formation and training, you will almost certainly gain a new academic qualification, probably at degree level. For some candidates this will be the latest in a long string of such achievements, and may come easily. For others it will be a first, and it may represent an enormous mountain to climb. Such qualifications are an important part of equipping for ministry – but they are not the only part. It can be true that those with the keenest brains for academic excellence will find some difficulty with the important tasks of self-reflection, or the empathetic seeing through the eyes of another. Nevertheless, understanding the wider context of theological reflection, which becomes possible through academic study, is also essential in the task of escaping from the limitations of our own perceptions.

Many colleges and courses offer a variety of degree and diploma programmes. The entry requirements for these courses reflect the varying background of candidates. Those training to diploma level in the pre-ordination course may be able to use their continuing ministerial education (CME – see Chapter 6) to build up to a full honours degree. Others will achieve an honours degree, a master's or a research degree through their training. The new proposals for training in the Church of England should introduce new possibilities to go on with accredited study in the early years of ministry.

Finding a curacy

About one year before ordination is expected to take place, the process of finding a curacy will begin. The initial stage of this final part of the path towards ordained ministry begins with the interim report from the training institution. (The final report – in which the college or course principal may recommend or not recommend for ordination – comes right at the end of the training.) The tutors prepare this interim report in careful consultation with each student, so that an accurate assessment of their gifts, growth and learning goals is provided.

The report is sent to the sponsoring bishop and the DDO, together with a simple form on which the student indicates their preferences and needs in a training post. These will include the social and church context – in other words, urban or rural, or shades between, and high or low church. It also allows the student to indicate housing needs, reflecting family circumstances, and gives the opportunity to express a preference for staying within or moving out of the sponsoring diocese. The form does not always seem to allow for easy expression of preferences – it's a good idea to leave options as open as reasonably and sensibly possible, with brief glossing comments if necessary.[4]

Bishops are discouraged from making suggestions about possible training positions before these reports are received from the training institutions in June or July. Once the reports have been received for all the candidates from a particular diocese, the bishop's senior staff meeting will discuss possible positions. In making suggestions, priority is given – in theory – to the training needs of the candidate and the training abilities of the potential incumbent. This has not always been apparent in the final decisions made, but it is increasingly becoming so. As with earlier parts of the process, this is ideally a collaborative exercise – although there are limitations to this collaboration, arising either from confidential knowledge in the diocese of personal circumstances, or from national quotas, which can lead to an unhelpful sense of disempowering to those who have made very real sacrifices to arrive at this stage of their lives.

Non-stipendiary curacies

Candidates for non-stipendiary ministry will not normally be expecting to move home, and so options for their deployment will be limited. As with other areas of training, policies vary from diocese to diocese with regard to whether candidates will be permitted to be ordained to their sponsoring parish. Some bishops feel that a change of air and perspective is necessary, whilst others are prepared to accept the frequently expressed desire of candidates – especially older candidates – to minister in the congregation that has fostered and provided the immediate context for their vocation.

It may come as a surprise to you to learn that non-stipendiary ministers (NSMs) are expected to work under the same discipline of obedience to the bishop as those who are paid: they are, after all, just as much representatives of the whole Church as those who are stipendiary, and they carry the same authority, so it is inevitable that they must work within the same discipline. Working agreements (see below) are especially important for NSM curates: these set out mutual expectations between training incumbent and curate, so that each knows what may be expected of themselves and the other. It is especially important during the training period for NSM ministers not to come and go as they please – although this may feel unduly oppressive to the unpaid candidate.

Stipendiary candidates

Stipendiary candidates owe their first allegiance to their sponsoring diocese. The diocese has supported them spiritually and probably financially (if they have a family) through training, and will normally make the first offer of a training position for the candidate to consider. Some dioceses are recognized as 'exporting': they customarily sponsor more candidates through training than they have training positions available for, and they may be willing from the outset for candidates to look elsewhere for a first post. This will often have been made clear when a candidate had their initial conversations with the DDO.

Candidates from a diocese that has not given them this early release will need to wait to be contacted by the bishop or DDO in the early summer to discover what may be suggested for them. This may be an anxious time: although it is the focus for the long process of selection and training, the all-encompassing nature of a curate's work, touching not only professional but the whole of domestic life as well, means that the stakes are higher than for many secular jobs where it is possible to separate work and home life to a much greater degree. What will the house be like? The schools? The neighbourhood? The incumbent? The church? What pattern – what expectation – has been set by any predecessors?

You may well have a conversation, face to face or over the telephone, or you may just get a letter to introduce the profile of the parish where it is suggested that you continue your training. It is very rare for a candidate simply to be asked to 'go and have a chat with Revd Smith – that could be a good place for you', now that, following guidelines from the Ministry Division, the incumbent is required to produce a parish profile.

The parish that is first suggested to you needs to be given your careful consideration. Those who know your needs and the possibilities within the diocese have considered that this could be a good place for you both to make a contribution to the ministry and to receive a good training for the future. It is not, however, your only option! Should you decide that it is not the right place for you, the diocese may have other suggestions, or there will be other opportunities elsewhere in the country which you will be able to explore in due course, as we explain below.

Will there be a job for me? – how posts are distributed across the country

There is a nationally agreed allocation of training posts which ensures a fair distribution of new clergy across all the dioceses. The formula governing this allocation was originally proposed by a working party chaired by the Bishop of Sheffield, and has since become known as the 'clergy share formula'. It is the governing principle for appointments, particularly in the early stages of matching candidates with parishes.

Vocation and guidance: how do I know if this is the 'right' place?

Making a choice of ministry post may seem both practically and theoretically complicated! It is practically complicated because so many people seem to be involved in making the decision – and because it's not always clear what the options are to those who are most directly involved: the candidates themselves. It is theoretically complicated because the basis for making a decision is clearly far more than 'Does it pay well?', or even 'Would I enjoy it?', but strays into the relatively uncharted areas of sacrifice, calling and 'What does God want?' At its most extreme, it can feel like the need to discern *the* one right position that God has marked down for you. If you can spot it, all will be well; if you don't, nothing will ever go right.

It is true that God is intimately associated with the choices that we make, and that he has called us into ministry. The initial identification of this calling, discussed in the last chapter, was called discernment – a word that implies a mixture of conscious and intuitive observation and judgement, with the deliberate invocation of the guidance of the Holy Spirit, to arrive at a way of seeing through God's eyes. The same process needs to be brought into play when examining potential curacy positions.

God's 'will' should perhaps best be seen as 'God's possibilities', rather than as a single right or wrong option. He is able to take our offered lives and talents and use them in many different ways to build his kingdom: any one of a number of different routes can, once we have committed to it, become the way that God will weave us into his wider work. He uses us as we are, including our history, our strengths and our weaknesses, often making connections with others that in retrospect seem almost planned, but which actually could have worked out in many different ways.

So, when approaching a possible curacy, we should avoid the temptation to abdicate personal responsibility in a blind search for God's perfect guidance. It is certainly important to pray, however, and to seek to be open to all possibilities. Guidance is above all a matter of learning to see as God sees, and this emerges primarily through two things: practice and community. The practice will include refining our own ability to see, to read a situation – to look below the surface, to read between the lines. It will also include growing in wisdom as to how God is at work in the world – through an increasing knowledge of Scripture and the Christian tradition, and through the relating of this in dialogue with our own analysis of the world we see around us. It will include the living into and out of our tentative conclusions, as we ask 'How is God at work in the world, and how can I be a partner with him?' (This is the process known as theological reflection: a fancy name for something that we all do, consciously or not.) This process, though, requires community to be built on a secure foundation. If I do not see the world through the eyes of others as well as my own, my vision will be sadly deficient. If I do not reflect in conversation with others, my views will be unbalanced and lacking perspective. As we grow in these disciplines, we will grow in our ability to discern God's will.

Guidance may come through an apparently miraculous intervention. There are many examples of these: the place we are considering might appear three times in as many hours on TV screens, newspapers, passing lorries as we are asking God to let us know what he wants us to do, for example. It's foolish to dismiss as completely irrelevant such incidents, or the more obviously directive 'prophetic words' that may be offered in some Christian contexts. However, they should not be treated as prescriptive, fortune-telling predictions, but rather as an invitation to think with God about how he may be speaking to us in all the ways that he has given us to recognize the possibilities set before us.

It is especially important to avoid the assumption that the route that involves the most suffering is the one that God must want us to take . . . or avoid! There are strong theological traditions present in the Church that would lead us to one or the other of these conclusions. 'Taking up our cross' to serve Christ is about taking on the role to which we are called, not about deliberately sacrificing ourselves.

A good basis for discerning how God may be calling us to serve him is found in Matthew 11.28-30: 'Come to me, all you that are weary and are carrying heavy burdens, and I will give you rest. Take my yoke upon you, and learn from me, for I am gentle and humble in heart, and you will find rest for your souls. For my yoke is easy, and my burden is light.' This verse is recalled by some priests in the Anglo-Catholic tradition as they kiss the stole before putting it on: it is a reminder that the ministry that we exercise is not just Christ's – it is, like a handmade wooden yoke, made to fit each minister exactly.

There has been some criticism in recent years of a growth in 'designer ministry': curates who insist that the position found for them must fit their individual needs, rather than their adjusting to the requirements of the church. It is true that we do not enter the ministry to satisfy our own needs. However, the nature of the ordained ministry is that it should fit the shape of the individual. It is not, after all, especially financially rewarding – it is a particular way of offering everything that we are to the work of God's kingdom. It demands all –not just of the individual, but of their family and often their friends as well – and so should as far as possible reflect the nature of each individual's gifts and circumstances.

All this means, as will probably be quite clear, that the candidate must look carefully and realistically at how she or he will 'fit' with the proposed parish, and whether there is that spark of excitement that says, 'With God, we could really go somewhere together'. It has often been observed that choosing a parish is similar to choosing a marriage partner: it is tempting to think that, once married, it will be possible to 'change' one's partner into the perfect spouse. The truth is that the change does not always follow – our decision must be made on the basis of what the other partner is like now.

Assessing a potential position

How can a candidate 'read' a parish – look below the surface to discern what is really going on, and whether they would be able to play a positive part within it? I remember being urged to compare the published attendance figures with the numbers actually present on the Sunday when I visited – it was good advice! Rather like two men talking on the way to a squash match, there are always a host of reasons offered as to why this particular occasion will not match up to the norm!

The parish profile or statement

The parish profile will reveal much of what the parish would like to be – and something of what it is. What it would like to be is significant, even if this is as yet unrealized, because this is the goal towards which the potential curate may be invited to work, in partnership with the existing team.

Useful questions to bear in mind when reading the parish statement might include:

- What is the curate's role?

  - in relation to the incumbent (colleague, junior colleague, co-worker; close, distant . . .)

  - in relation to the adult church members

  - in relation to the children and young people (be wary of assumptions that the curate will operate as the youth worker)

  - in relation to the parish community – those who live in the area but are not members of the church

  - in relation to the wider Church – the diocese, etc.

- Are there particular expectations of the curate? Too many, and the candidate may feel swamped; too few, and the candidate may feel that their contribution will not be valued, or that they will have 'no role' at all.

- What is the model of ministry in the parish: collaborative, or clergy do all? Is a distinctive ministry envisaged for the clergy? Lack of clarity on this can be the downfall of many training relationships. The Dean of Westminster Abbey, Wesley Carr, explains that 'everyone associated with a church . . . has their own mental image of what it is, what it is for and how it works', but that these images can be quite different. In his *Handbook of Pastoral Studies* he describes four different models of church which will be familiar to many theological students, each of which emphasizes a different aspect of ministry and understands the church's structure and leadership in different ways. In the church as 'Herald', for example, the primary task of the church is understood as the proclamation of the gospel, and the preaching ministry will be given prominence. In the church as 'Servant', the preaching ministry of the church, and therefore of the minister, will not be emphasized. In the other models Carr describes, 'Sacrament' and 'Body of Christ', the role of the priest takes a different form again.[5] It is therefore worth exploring with the incumbent their understanding of the role of a priest/minister in the church you are looking at.

- Does the parish respect people, or is it driven by programmes . . . or is it so concerned for people that it seems to have no programme at all? Does it sound as if clergy are treated as human beings?

- Does the church ministry seem to represent the community in which it is set – and if not, what does that say to you positively, about opportunities for development, or negatively, about the dangers of an inward-looking fellowship?

It can be helpful to follow the structure of a SWOT analysis, looking at the apparent Strengths, Weaknesses, Opportunities and Threats that are present. This may reveal places where you feel you could make a contribution, or places where your contribution might initially appear superfluous.

Most churches have a ministry that is based not just in one particular church tradition, but in a particular understanding of the gospel – which might broadly and simplistically be expressed as inclusive or exclusive, often determined according to a criterion of declared faith. It may be possible to discover a church's approach to ministry through a mission statement, or its calendar of services and meetings, or by the range of its membership. *Studying Congregations: A New Handbook*[6] offers very helpful resources for exploring the theology of a congregation, in particular the way in which it may say one thing and actually model another. Who, for example, are the congregation's 'heroes of the faith'? It may be that a church which professes one tradition will widely recognize as an exemplar someone who is from quite a different tradition: someone who does not subscribe to an accepted basis of faith, perhaps, or who draws spiritual sustenance from a tradition that is not otherwise present in the church. As with models of leadership, it is important for a candidate to know what they are getting into – diverse models of ministry can be enriching, or they can lead to relationship tensions and even breakdown.

Above all, it is probably important to ask, 'Am I excited by what I have read?' If there is no sense of pull, beware: it might mean that you would not have taken this any further if you had not been asked to consider it.

As has already been said, a curacy is much more than a job. It will provide the context for your whole life, and that of any family who move with you. The house details are important, as may be the schools, and access to leisure facilities. Reactions to these elements of the profile – both yours and your family's – are every bit as significant as to the job. You should not view the personal provision as unimportant!

It can often be worthwhile for candidates to ask someone else to look over the parish profile, pointing out anything that occurs to them about how the candidate might fit (or not) into what they have read, or suggesting important questions to ask during the visit.

Visiting the parish

You will need to arrange a visit to the prospective parish. Making the initial phone call can itself be daunting. It may be worth remembering that the incumbent will feel just as anxious as you do!

When you visit the parish, your focus needs to be upon the relationship the curate will have with the potential incumbent. Facts and figures, and even individuals in the parish, will change over time, and all will take second place to the training relationship. It is common for a visit to take place over a weekend, and you may well be offered hospitality in the vicarage, which is a good way of spending time together. If you are married, take your partner with you if at all possible: a second opinion is invaluable, and the move is not just for you, but for your family as well.

Candidates sometimes say, 'What should I ask?' It is probably most important to ask *yourself* questions whilst on the visit: 'Could I worship here?'; 'Do I respect his/her opinion?'; 'Can we pray together?' Candidates who are accustomed to praying with others may find it important to be able to pray with colleagues. It is in praying with another that we make ourselves vulnerable, and reveal our true priorities: an unwillingness to do this may ring alarm bells about the nature of a working relationship.

Visiting a parish is an opportunity for mutual testing: both incumbent and candidate are inviting the other to look carefully at them and make judgements. This can feel daunting, and even inappropriate. It is, of course, important to try to be honest: mistakes made at this stage can produce bitter fruit some months down the line.

It may be possible when visiting a parish to begin to discern the nature of the relationship between the incumbent and the members of the church or local community. It is good to have the opportunity to spend time with them on their own. A good potential incumbent will enable this to happen, aware that others' perspective is necessary for a candidate to make a decision.

The key relationship in any parish is that between the incumbent and the curate: and this relationship will have a profound impact on both parties. You should consider carefully the incumbent's response to your visit as a mirror of your own hopes and anxieties. Just as you as a candidate may wonder what you can bring to the parish, so an incumbent may wonder what they can offer an experienced candidate. Both parties should be looking for what they can receive, as well as offer, in the relationship.

Specific questions to ask

A checklist for the interview with the potential supervising incumbent may include:

- How will the incumbent encourage the curate's
    - time off: days and holidays
    - need to care for family/spend time with friends
    - further study/research
    - further training
    - retreat
    - membership of a cell group?

- What will the incumbent's attitude be to:
    - the curate's attendance at parish events – would you need to be at everything/most things, etc?
    - the ministry of your partner/children?

- How do they model these things themselves?

- What practical support is available to the curate – e.g. secretarial assistance?

- What is the curate's role in decision-making in the parish?

- How often does the team meet? What opportunities will there be for incumbent and curate supervision?

- Have they had a curate before, and if not, are they prepared for a steep learning curve?

- Does the incumbent think you'll be like them?

- How will they train you – what's their approach likely to be? Will they want to check your sermons before you preach?

- Have they seen the report from college – and do they want to say anything about it? Do you want to show it to them?

- How does the incumbent relax?

- What plans are there for developing the church's ministry – and what might be your place within that? To have a project to develop yourself can be a very valuable part of training.

You will want to look at the house – and be prepared to ask difficult questions. If promises are made about future provision, make sure you have them in writing for the sake of clear agreement, especially if a house has yet to be bought.

You will want to ask yourself: 'Is the job/parish profile true?'

It is hard to know whether or not to press difficult questions, especially if you sense that they might concern areas of potential conflict, for example homosexuality, universalism, women bishops. Nevertheless, although the specific issues may not be worth falling out over at this stage, it will be important to assess how you might handle disagreement in a shared ministry.[7]

What is the interviewing incumbent thinking?

The interviewing incumbent is likely to be enthusiastic about receiving a curate. This may be because they enjoy having a colleague, or because they appreciate the challenges of training. It is also likely that they will value an extra pair of hands – though the priority in arranging curacies is ostensibly the training needs of the newly ordained, the practical demands of ministry are never far away.

The incumbent may find themselves talking to a potential colleague at the request of the bishop, or because they have been approached by a candidate who has read the parish profile. In either case, they will want to know if they will be able to work well together. What matters to this person about their ministry? What is it that brings them alive when they talk about the future? They will want to know about the candidate's former experience, both in the life of the Church and more broadly – to listen to them talk about it, and to discover how they might bring that experience into their new life to enrich the ministry of the whole parish. As they listen to the candidate talk about their own personal needs and aspirations, they will be looking for a match between these and the needs and aspirations of the parish.

The interviewing incumbent, like the candidate, will want to accept the recommendation of the bishop if at all possible. There will be a real anxiety in the incumbent's mind that if they do not accept the recommended candidate, there might not be another option – and in spite of the desire to find a good fit, this may sway their judgement. Nevertheless, they will be hoping for a genuine personal chemistry which suggests that collaboration will be enriched by diversity, there will be an easy shared life of prayer, and mutual challenge will be present and welcomed. They are likely to be looking for a candidate who is happy to work with the church's and the incumbent's tradition even if they do not share it themselves.

How to make a decision

It is easy to say that decision-making is about listening to your head and listening to your heart – but hearing what's being said may be difficult! It will be important to pray and reflect, but also to talk through your reactions with other people, since this will help you to clarify how you think and feel about all you have seen. Judging where God's prompting may lie is best done corporately.

The decision is not yours alone, and it may be that the incumbent or the parish will invite you to come but that you feel less certain. Perhaps you think they haven't understood you, or for some other reason you don't believe there's a sufficiently good 'fit'. As has already been said, it's necessary to get the right balance between considering 'what's right for me' and asking 'Where am I called to serve?' – ministry does involve sacrificing the priority of our own comforts, but it should not ride roughshod over who we are.

On the other hand, the candidate may be full of enthusiasm and respond with pain and confusion when a parish says 'No'. Strangely, this often happens to candidates who appear to have a great deal to offer: it should not be seen as an indication of unsuitability for ministry! In this situation the candidate will need to take a little time to gather themselves together before continuing to look for the place where the 'fit' is right. The emotional investment necessary to explore a post is taxing, and will take some time to unravel. Discerning vocation inevitably involves a thinking (and feeling) oneself into 'What would it be like to live and work here?' Moving into and out of this needs to be done gently.

If both incumbent and candidate agree that they should go ahead, formal letters need to be exchanged in which the candidate is offered the post by the incumbent and the candidate accepts the offer. The agreement of the diocese should be checked at every stage, and this also will need confirming in writing before the post is formally offered to the candidate.

What happens if I turn them down or they turn me down?

Some candidates will happily, and rightly, accept the first post that is offered to them. For many, however, it is only after looking at one post that they are able to clarify their own thinking about what they are really looking for. There is no stigma attached to this, and the process anticipates that there will be many who will take some time to discover an appropriate first parish.

The diocese may make subsequent suggestions, or it may be at this stage that a candidate is 'released' to look elsewhere.

Candidates who are 'released', and those unplaced by November

If the bishop decides that he is not able to offer a candidate a training post in his diocese, he will ask the DDO to contact them to 'release' them to look elsewhere. Until this takes place, candidates are obligated to their sponsoring diocese. Such release may come at a very early stage in training, especially in dioceses with very large numbers of ordinands. It is more usual, however, for it to come in the summer preceding the anticipated year of ordination. The diocese may come to this decision as soon as it sits down with all the information about its candidates to hand, or it may come on a case-by-case basis as the summer proceeds.

The manner of communicating this information is a sensitive issue. DDOs often have heavy workloads, and in the interest of passing on information as quickly as possible, some telephone candidates with the news. This can feel lackadaisical: 'they couldn't even be bothered to give me a proper letter telling me they don't want me' is a common reaction. Alternatively, a letter may be greeted with the response, 'they couldn't even be bothered to speak to me personally'! The impact of release needs to be handled carefully by the DDO: however much a candidate may want to be free to look anywhere in the country, the news that your home no longer has a place for you will always be a hard message to hear. Whatever the initial means of communication, the decision must be confirmed in writing before candidates may consider themselves free to look outside of their sponsoring diocese for a title parish.

As has been said, some candidates will be 'released' at an early stage – perhaps in their first year of training – to look for a curacy anywhere in the country. Many bishops, however, like to consider their whole range of potential training parishes, and ordinands, before deciding who should be released. Candidates who have not finalized a position in their home diocese by 31 October of the year preceding the one in which they are due to be ordained are free to look anywhere in the country, and it is at this stage that the process of finding a curacy moves into a different gear. It is still possible for a candidate who has been officially released by their own diocese to apply for positions within that diocese, circulated as generally available through the same process as they would follow if exploring a position in any another diocese.

Looking for a curacy outside your home diocese

At the end of October, bishops send to the principals of the theological colleges and courses confirmation of which of their sponsored candidates they undertake to place within their diocese. (However, *all* candidates who by that stage have yet to finalize a training position are still free to look elsewhere: in spite of the diocese's best intentions, a successful match may not be found.) They also circulate details of possible training parishes to all the principals. The procedure for this is now carefully prescribed to ensure equal opportunities for all candidates who are looking for a title parish: details of positions should arrive with each principal by the same post. Once details have arrived, they are normally made available to all the students, who are able to phone the incumbent of a parish that sounds promising.

There are, of course, other ways in which candidates may come to hear of potential vacancies. A wide variety of personal conversations with friends or family, or meetings at conferences or other events, can lead to discussions of curacy possibilities. This is to be expected, but it is important that conversations arising from these contacts are checked out at a very early stage with senior diocesan staff and the principal of the college or course, so that hopes are not dashed against national or diocesan allocations of vacancies (which in some of the larger dioceses can apply to areas of a diocese as well as to the diocese as a whole).

The code of practice states that candidates may only explore one parish at a time, and that incumbents similarly may only enter into discussion with one candidate at a time. This is an unusual system, and one which can be deeply frustrating to both candidates and supervisors. In its defence, it is a way of preventing either candidates or incumbents from holding a handful of partners and clogging the system for other potential applicants. It can, however, make it quite difficult to make decisions: most people make decisions by weighing the alternatives, rather than by taking each possibility in isolation and saying 'Is this it?' The similarity with choosing a marriage partner, which we have already identified, is perhaps worth revisiting: the rightness of the choice is discovered in worked-out commitment. The full realization of what a place or partnership can mean will only emerge within the context of that commitment. Nevertheless, it can be a frustrating business, and parishes have been known to play one candidate against another. Similarly, candidates pursuing one parish who become aware of an alternative possibility midway through the process and find that it casts doubts upon their initial choice would do well to discuss their hesitations with the initial prospective incumbent. It may be important to continue to pursue the initial enquiry – but this may also be foolish and unhelpful to all concerned. The code of procedure does allow the possibility of looking at a second parish alongside the first if this has been discussed beforehand with the principal and the bishop or bishops concerned.

If a candidate discovers upon contacting a potential parish that someone else is already looking at that parish, they may wish to offer to send their details anyway in case the earlier enquiry should prove fruitless. This does not, of course, prevent them from looking elsewhere.

The process of looking at parishes identified through personal contact or details circulated to principals is identical to that described above.

The sponsoring diocese remains responsible for the candidate (and their family, where appropriate) until they are actually ordained in another diocese. It is accepted that this responsibility is shared with the principal of the training institution.

What happens if I can't find anywhere at all?

There are a variety of reasons why a candidate may find that the summer of their ordination is approaching and they have yet to identify a suitable training post. Their sponsoring diocese may not have suggested any possible parishes to them, or it may have made suggestions that proved unsatisfactory either to the candidate or to the potential incumbent: this will have released the diocese from its obligation to the candidate, who has been free (or been required) to look elsewhere. A diocese may have made it clear at an early stage of the process that for reasons of numbers it is unable to provide a training position. The exception to this is for those for whom the bishop overruled the recommendation of the selection conference and chose to sponsor a candidate against the selectors' advice: in this situation, the bishop is bound to find a training position for the candidate.

In January of the anticipated year of ordination, the Ministry Division takes a new responsibility for unplaced candidates. Details of unplaced candidates and unfilled vacancies are circulated nationally. This happens again in March. Ultimately, dioceses or diocesan areas that have been unable to fill allocated places may release such positions to the national or diocesan pool.

It may be, however, that a candidate is simply unable to find a parish or incumbent to which they feel they can commit themselves. Each year there are a few people who find themselves in this position, in which case ordination has to be deferred. It is not possible to be ordained without a parish: ordination is to the Church within the context of a parish community. Candidates may defer either to Michaelmas (the end of September), or for a year or more.

It is always the case that some candidates identify a training parish at a late stage in the process, and that a small number defer for a few months or a year. Sometimes vacancies for training posts emerge unexpectedly as an existing curate moves late in the year. Sometimes a new incumbent is appointed who would be a good trainer, and so the parish becomes available for a training post. It is certainly not true that it is 'weak' candidates who are last to be placed.

A candidate who defers will usually find that they will become responsible for their own maintenance once the anticipated date for ordination has passed.

What happens if something goes wrong?

Occasionally, an incumbent moves or has some personal crisis which means that they are no longer able to receive a curate. This is of course very difficult for everybody concerned, and may mean that ordination has to be deferred for a year. In this situation, the diocese may take financial responsibility for the candidate: it may be that the candidate will spend a further year in training as a way of making good use of their time, and to enable a suitable alternative training post to be found.

Clergy couples

There are now a significant number of couples in training for ministry. Diocesan policies in relation to clergy couples vary widely: some are supportive of couples training in the same parish, most are not. There is also a wide variation in stipendiary provision for couples: some dioceses will offer stipends to both partners, others will not expect to offer this. Guidelines on the deployment and remuneration of clergy couples have been prepared by the Ministry Division.

Styles of ministry preferred by clergy couples are very varied. Some would choose to work together if possible, others entirely separately. Finding a place where each will be able to express their own ministry, and explore the possibilities of collaborative work, is very important. The rewards of ministry for clergy couples are huge; so are the pitfalls, especially from sharing a house that is simultaneously a place of work. American research has confirmed the high incidence of marriage breakdown in clergy couples: safeguards must be built in at an early stage, and expectations from parishes should be especially carefully examined.[8]

The pre-ordination retreat and the ordination service

As the initial training moves to completion, so the ordination service begins to loom: a key moment for every candidate and for their friends and family. Some will look forward to it with eager anticipation, others with dread.[9]

All candidates will go on an ordination retreat, which is organized by the diocese. This is usually residential and normally begins on the Thursday prior to the ordination on the Sunday. Ordinations themselves take place on the Sunday closest to the feast of St Peter and St Paul, which falls on 29 June. There is always a rehearsal for the service, which often leads into the retreat for the candidates. Indeed, some dioceses consider the rehearsal to be the beginning of the retreat: as the candidates gather in the centre of the cathedral, they engage in a new way with the reality of the changes that are soon to take place, and upon which they will reflect in the coming two or three days. The rehearsal is also valuable in that the embarrassment of walking around in unfamiliar robes and roles can be shared and overcome.

The retreat can be a confusing time for the family and friends of a candidate, especially for a family that has just moved to a new house. Most retreats include periods of silence, and the sense of being out of touch with the candidate can add to the perception of loss of control and loss of relationship as the candidate is whisked away into the secret and 'magical' land of the clergy. For the candidate, it is an opportunity to pause, relax, pray, and make relationships with their new diocesan colleagues; for the family it may be a frantic time of getting the house ready to receive guests without the help of one of the key players. It may be useful for the family to plan to take the time as their own mini retreat or break, before they begin this new stage of their life together.

Two elements of the retreat are worthy of particular attention: the possibility of 'confession', and the oaths of obedience. Both may be unfamiliar, and threatening – but both provide important opportunities for reflection and commitment. Most retreat conductors will offer candidates the chance to have a personal interview, and this will include the possibility of sacramental confession. Some candidates will be familiar with this discipline, and be accustomed to taking advantage of the opportunity it gives for careful reflection, assurance of forgiveness, and recommitment. For others, it provides a way in to one of the most helpful maintenance checks available to Christians. It is both encouraging and liberating, and forms a natural and beneficial part of the retreat.

The oaths of obedience that the candidate is required to make before the ordination may also produce an uncertain reaction. How is it that we are asked to take into our hands a New Testament, which includes an injunction against swearing on anything, to affirm our allegiance to the officers of the institution of

Church and state? Our reactions to this apparent contradiction need examining carefully: the presenting issue may actually simply be a cover for our uncertainty about the commitment embodied in the oaths. The commitment in the oaths is in truth two-way: not only is it a commitment to Christ in the Church on the part of the candidate, it mirrors, and is a way of receiving, the commitment of the Church to the candidate which will be expressed only a little later in the service of ordination.

The ordination service may pass in a blur for the candidates and their supporters. Within it are readings from scripture that affirm the ministry of the whole people of God, and the particular calling of those set apart for public ministry. The candidates are first presented to the bishop, and then by him to the people present, to seek their corporate affirmation and promise of support for this new ministry. The candidates themselves are asked to affirm and commit themselves afresh to God, the church, and their calling. In a poignant moment, the whole assembly kneels in silence, and then sings or says a prayer to the Holy Spirit for anointing for ministry. After further prayer for the candidates and the church, each comes in turn to kneel before the bishop who lays hands upon their heads, with the prayer:

> Send down the Holy Spirit upon your servant *N* for the office and work of a deacon [*or* priest] in your Church.

Candidates are dressed in their stoles, and a New Testament (for deacons) or Bible (for priests) is given to each one, 'as a sign of God's authority' to preach and to minister. Then there is the opportunity for the candidates and congregation to greet one another at the peace: this may be the first time the candidate has spoken to their family and friends since leaving for the retreat.

In the first part of the service, there is a description of the work of deacons, and priests, read by the bishop to the candidates. It is appropriate to end this chapter with these words, which stand as a touchstone for those either considering or looking back on ordination, as they pray through their calling to ministry:

> A *deacon* is called to serve the Church of God, and to work with its members in caring for the poor, the needy, the sick, and all who are in trouble. He is to strengthen the faithful, search out the careless and the indifferent, and to preach the word of God in the place to which he is licensed. A deacon assists the priest under whom he serves, in leading the worship of the people, especially in the administration of the Holy Communion. He may baptize when required to do so. It is his general duty to do such pastoral work as is entrusted to him.

A *priest* is called by God to work with the bishop and with his fellow-priests, as servant and shepherd among the people to whom he is sent. He is to proclaim the word of the Lord, to call his hearers to repentance, and in Christ's name to absolve and to declare the forgiveness of sins. He is to baptize and prepare the baptized for Confirmation. He is to preside at the celebration of the Holy Communion. He is to lead his people in prayer and worship, to intercede for them, to bless them in the name of the Lord, and to teach and encourage by word and example. He is to minister to the sick, and prepare the dying for their death. He must set the Good Shepherd always before him as the pattern of his calling, caring for the people committed to his charge, and joining with them in a common witness to the world.

In the name of our Lord we bid you remember the greatness of the trust now to be committed to your charge, about which you have been taught in your preparation for this ministry. You are to be messengers, watchmen, and stewards of the Lord; you are to teach and to admonish, to feed and to provide for the Lord's family, to search for his children in the wilderness of this world's temptations and to guide them through its confusions, so that they may be saved through Christ for ever.

Remember always with thanksgiving that the treasure now to be entrusted to you is Christ's own flock, bought through the shedding of his blood on the cross. The Church and congregation among whom you will serve are one with him: they are his body. Serve them with joy, build them up in faith, and do all in your power to bring them to loving obedience to Christ.

Because you cannot bear the weight of this ministry in your own strength but only by the grace and power of God, pray earnestly for his Holy Spirit. Pray that he will each day enlarge and enlighten your understanding of the Scriptures, so that you may grow stronger and more mature in your ministry, as you fashion your life and the lives of your people on the word of God.

We trust that long ago you began to weigh and ponder all this, and that you are fully determined, by the grace of God, to give yourselves wholly to his service and devote to him your best powers of mind and spirit, so that, as you daily follow the rule and teaching of our Lord, with the heavenly assistance of his Holy Spirit, you may grow up into his likeness, and sanctify the lives of all with whom you have to do.

4

Inner self: the 'being' of being a curate

Vanessa Herrick

I   'Who do people say that I am?': identifying issues

Introduction

> It was 6.30 a.m. on a summer Sunday morning. They had to leave
> for the cathedral by 7.30 so there wasn't much time. She got out
> of bed, had a quick shower and then started to get dressed. Her
> new suit hung tidily in the wardrobe, but first the shirt ... and
> then the collar. She struggled to squeeze the long strip of stiff
> white plastic into its slot, and glanced in the mirror to check
> that it was in properly. For a moment she stopped, surprised,
> distracted even by the sight of the stranger looking back at her.
> Then the need to get ready overtook her and she continued to
> get dressed. Yet in that passing instant the question hovered,
> unspoken, unacknowledged: 'Who do people say that I am?' – and
> in this echo of Christ's words to his disciples lay the seeds of a
> question of identity that would haunt her for years to come.

For most ordinands, their ordination day is a whirlwind of activity and emotion,
charged with joy, anxiety, expectation, awe and excitement. It is a day when they,
and those who are to be ordained deacon or priest alongside them, become a
focus of hope and expectation for the present and future ministry of the Church.
They have journeyed long and hard to get to this point and now the day has
come for their vocation to ordained ministry to be confirmed through the laying
on of hands. It is a significant day – at all sorts of levels, as the glance in the

mirror testifies. Being ordained – both the action and the condition – confers a shift, real and perceived, in the way in which we may understand ourselves and be understood by those around us. The effect of looking in the mirror and seeing a stranger with a dog collar is but the first sign of a tussle that may occupy the ordained throughout their ministries, but particularly in the early years. 'Now that I wear this collar, and take on all the expectations that go with it, who am I really, and who do people think I am?' Yet these are questions of identity that are rarely put into words: it is easier – and often necessary – simply to get on with the job.

Time to be

So much about being a curate is about doing: it is about school assemblies, sick communions, hospital visiting, drawing up rotas, preparing and preaching sermons, leading intercessions, running home groups, organizing events, baptism and wedding preparation, funeral visits, attending meetings – and so one could go on. There is nothing wrong with that, and it can often feel like a healthy antidote to the hours spent in lectures and group work during training. Yet, however naturally reflective a curate might be, and however good a training incumbent might be at encouraging their colleague to slow down and take time to think, there rarely seems room in a day, a week, or even a year to ask the questions 'Who am I?', and 'How is this role shaping me and how am I shaping it?' Such questions came into focus for one ordinand on a retreat I was leading:

Ben was enjoying his retreat. It had been wonderfully relaxing and a great chance to catch up on lost sleep. On the day before the ordination, he was wandering around the garden with one of his contemporaries. They were supposed to be in silence, but he found himself desperate to say to his fellow deacon: 'Here I am, the day before my priesting, and I'm not really sure I know who I am. I'm curate at St Bartholomew's, I'm Ann's husband and Tom and Stephen's dad, but it feels as if I've been on some sort of moving walkway, carried along through the years of selection and training and my deacon's year, without really having a chance to get off and think.'

For Ben, it was a significant moment. His was a 'good' curacy: he was really enjoying it, but nobody had helped him to reflect on what the experience was doing to him as a person. There had been lots of useful tips in CME 1–4, and lots of opportunity to compare notes and methodology with his fellow curates; there had even been some good theological debate and some

> interesting speakers. Yet nobody had helped him to think about who he was and what 'being ordained' might or might not be doing to him. He did not want to indulge in self-centred navel-gazing; he simply wanted the chance to reflect upon what might be going on inside.

Taking time to be is an essential part of being ordained – and not just for curates. When Jesus was facing times of transition or especially demanding situations or decisions, he went into the hills or other deserted places to pray. We hear of him trying to escape the crowds and withdrawing across the water, or to the sanctuary of his close friends at Bethany. After his baptism, before calling his disciples, on the Mount of Transfiguration, at the Last Supper and in the agony of Gethsemane – these were all moments of significance when Jesus himself needed to step back from the fray and try to recover some sense of who he was and what was happening. For it was in these moments of communion, of reconnecting with his heavenly Father through the Holy Spirit and with his closest friends and followers, that Jesus was able to find a point of security and stability that freed him to serve. He needed to know *who* he was, and *whose* he was, before he could carry on. In short, his identity was formed by his relationships, divine and human, and so is ours – but we need to take time to 'be' if we are going to discover what that identity is.[1]

Who I am versus what I do

A group of curates was once asked to complete a sentence beginning 'I am …'. Some responded with words like 'determined', 'caring', 'patient', 'warm-hearted', 'sometimes anxious', 'stubborn', and so on. Here, 'I am' evoked a response in terms of character and personality. Others responded in a different way: 'a woman', 'a mother', 'a wife', 'a friend', 'a journalist', 'a gardener', and so on. Here, 'I am' evoked a response in terms of role and relationship.

Most people, of course, would respond with a combination of the two, and it would be foolish to force an absolute distinction: the sort of person we are is affected by the relationships we have had and continue to have. Equally, there are times when we have to respond by doing things 'in role' in ways that are expected of us but may not come naturally! What becomes apparent is that 'role' and 'expectation' (of ourselves and others) can be a significant element in making us who we are – or at least, in making us who we present ourselves to be.[2]

This raises the classic question of the extent to which we are who we are by virtue of something intrinsic to our nature – a compilation and expression of the genes and particles that form our substance – and the extent to which we are who we are by virtue of the relationships in which we operate, with the possibility that those relationships themselves are, to some degree, shaped and determined by the roles each of us plays within them.

When we come to think about all this in relation to the 'being' of being a curate, we are forced to recognize the complexity of trying to work out who we are (and who we become) when we are ordained and take on that role. Undoubtedly, different curates will have different answers, affected – to a greater or lesser degree – by their theology of ordination. Indeed, the 'I am . . . ' exercise is an interesting one for curates to do because it quickly highlights the way in which they perceive themselves: as defined primarily by what sort of person they are, or by their role and their relationship with others.[3] Even the order in which the responses emerge may be significant and can occasionally betray what (consciously or unconsciously) they consider to be the most important and significant aspects of their lives! This complexity is, of course, not the preserve of the clerical profession: it exists for everybody to some degree, and especially for those who hold a role in public life. What matters is that these questions of 'being' are not ignored completely as those who are recently ordained grow into their work.[4]

For Jesus, being and doing, role and relationship, were all held together in his person. Yet in his public ministry, those around him were constantly questioning his identity, trying to see whether he matched up to their expectations, testing him, endeavouring to prove whether or not this carpenter's son from Nazareth could possibly be the Saviour of the world. So when he asked the disciples, 'Who do people say that the Son of Man is?' and 'Who do you say that I am?' (Matthew 16.13,15), it was not because he doubted his own identity, but because he genuinely wanted to know what those around him were thinking. Perhaps it was part of his testing of whether (as John would put it) 'his hour had yet come'. Jesus may have been fully aware of who he was, but he still needed to know how others perceived him. For as we shall see, it is sometimes perception rather than reality that is the problem.

It would be naïve to try to superimpose our own experience onto that of Jesus Christ, or vice versa. Nevertheless, the Gospels do seem to indicate that Jesus was the object of the competing expectations and perceptions of those around him. As eternal Son of the Father, he knew who he was; as an itinerant rabbi from Galilee, he may well, from time to time, have wondered! There was, perhaps, a genuine curiosity in his question, 'Who do people say that I am?' It is a question that curates may seriously want to ask themselves.

Clergy dress

These questions of identity come into sharp focus in relation to clerical dress. We began this section with the story of a woman getting dressed on the morning of her ordination. For her, as for many curates after her, the sight of herself wearing a dog collar for the first time was significant – although perhaps she did not realize just how significant at that moment. For the wearing of clergy dress, whether clerical collar or robes, continues to be one of the key factors in determining people's expectations, assumptions and attitudes towards the ordained. In the 'good old days' of the mid-twentieth century, it was possible to determine the churchmanship (sic) of a clergyman by the depth of his dog collar: the broader the collar, the more evangelical he would be! Similarly, the quantity of lace on a cotta might be a sign of a clergyman's 'position' on the Anglo-Catholic spectrum.

It is not only within the fashion-conscious world of the Church that such things have significance, however. As the newly ordained quickly discover, wearing a dog collar can cause some unusual and unexpected reactions amongst the general public – even on the day of ordination – as one of our curates was to discover:

> They had just finished clearing away the post-ordination picnic and Tom needed to collect his robes from the cathedral. He was keen to get home for a cup of tea before setting out again for the evening 'Welcome Service' in the parish church. As he crossed the market square, an elderly woman smiled at him and said, 'Good afternoon!' As he entered the car park, a man in his twenties came up to him and asked the way to the local community centre. Tom was surprised: he wasn't used to people smiling or talking to him in the street . . .

Somehow, the flash of white plastic had made people feel safe. It can work the other way, however:

> I was once travelling to a meeting at Church House and had decided to wear my collar since there would be representatives from a number of community organizations present, and it would be helpful for people to know that I was from 'the Church'. The underground was reasonably busy, and there were only two free seats in the carriage – one on either side of me! On that occasion, somehow the collar got in the way.

Some ordained women find it hard to work out how to appear feminine and attractively dressed when a dog collar seems to turn them into some sort of 'neuter being'. Is it so wrong to want to look good in uniform? Yet for both genders, the dog collar can also be seen as extraordinarily attractive! It may come as something of a shock to the newly ordained, but the appeal of the white 'ring of confidence' can be surprisingly wide ranging.

Despite the strange effect it has on others, most clergy see the dog collar as a helpful 'passport' into conversations and situations where they might otherwise be unwelcome – or, at least, held in great suspicion. Others prefer not to wear one at all, believing them to be off-putting, especially to the younger generation.

What is clear is that a collar (or robes at a funeral or wedding, for example) signifies that a person is operating in a particular role for a particular purpose. Not that that makes them any less of a person, but it carries with it, implicitly at least, a framework for relating both for the clergy person and for those they are with. However out of touch the Church might be, it seems the dog collar still has a message of its own.

One of the difficulties with this, of course, is that there sometimes seems to be a gulf between who we know ourselves to be at any one time and the role that we are expected to fulfil. How do we go and lead a school assembly on being patient and forgiving when we've just 'kicked the cat', shouted at the children and had a row with our husband or wife? At such times a dog collar can feel like a chain around our neck: we want to be free of all these unrealistic expectations. Or what about those occasions when our behaviour feels incompatible with our own and other people's expectations? Some curates, for example, say that wearing a dog collar has improved their driving! They keep to the speed limit and drive less aggressively. Others may feel less positively constrained about expressing emotion or weakness.[5] So, how do we handle the dilemma? We may be extremely irritated with a parishioner; we may be desperately upset with a close friend and yet feel constrained about expressing any such emotion or weakness, uncertain whether to be true to ourselves or hide behind a mask.

It would seem that wearing a dog collar brings into focus the tension between the 'personal' and the 'professional', between who we are and what we would like to be. We are who we are with all our failings; and yet we are also expected to be and to act in a professional way. This is right and proper, but sometimes we simply don't get the balance right. It is surprising how one small piece of white plastic can make clergy – and curates especially – stop and think about who they are and how they are behaving. Perhaps that's not such a bad thing.

Jesus knew what it was to live with the unrealistic and erroneous expectations and assumptions of those around him. Sometimes he challenged them; often he didn't, but worked through their wrong assumptions to point them; to his Father and to the values of the kingdom. In Jesus' case, of course, there was no disjunction between who he was and who he appeared to be. His 'rabbi's robes' were not there to hide the reality underneath, but to enable him to speak and to demonstrate the truth of God's love for his people. We as clergy, however, know all too well that we are not all we may seem to be to the outside world; indeed, we may fall far short of the paradigm. Keeping a realistic perspective on ourselves is vital: it is easy to become so 'puffed up' with the success of our preaching or pastoral ministry that we lose sight of our human frailty. When we do, our ministry begins to lack integrity and we can get in the way of God and his purposes. When Jesus hung naked on the cross, the Father looked on in love and pain and pity: his obedient Son had nothing to hide, and everything to give. Our collars and our robes are but a frail covering hiding the weakness of our humanity from the world around us: when the Father looks on us, what does he see?

2   Great expectations: continuity and change in relationships

Introduction

Ordination affects expectations: of the ordained in respect of themselves, and of others in respect of those who are ordained. Often, those expectations are unspoken or hidden: they can be realistic or unrealistic, achievable or impractical. They can be expectations about conduct, ability or manner. They can be expectations about use of time, ways of relating and ways of reacting. They can be expectations that are not about the ordained person at all, but concern his or her family, home and leisure activities. Sometimes expectations are fair and reasonable, but often they are built on a historical, a false or a distorted understanding of what ordained ministry is about. Frequently, they veil the pains and disappointments of those who have both given and received the ministry of the ordained in years gone by. Expectations – ours and others' – are a very powerful force.

For curates, dealing with expectations can be particularly difficult as they not only learn to adjust to new patterns of working, new relationships, and very often a new working and living environment, but also as they begin to recognize the ways in which previously existing relationships are affected by their new status. There may be a good deal of continuity, but where changes in attitude are perceived, they can often be difficult to handle, for the expectations (and the assumptions that go with them) are often more than skin deep.

In the early days of a new post, many curates are, understandably, primarily concerned with the health of their relationship with their incumbent (this is discussed in more detail in Chapter 6). What concerns us here, however, are the other relationships that are significantly affected when a person becomes a curate, and yet which are rarely 'flagged up' in training or acknowledged during the course of a curacy – relationships which (perhaps even more than that with the incumbent) can determine the health and stability of the early years of ordained ministry. Many of the issues raised are common to married and single curates; some are unique to one or the other.

Relating to the family

Ordination affects the whole family, and Jesus' question in St Mark's Gospel, 'Who are my mother and my brothers?' (Mark 3.33), can seem all too real to those who feel abandoned by the one who has been ordained. The sense of dislocation (actual and metaphorical) and upheaval felt by the family can be immense. However supportive they have been through the periods of selection and training, however much they have talked with others in similar situations, however well the college or course has tried to prepare them – few can know what it's like to be a curate or a curate's spouse or close dependant until it happens; and it is often the changes in expectations that can be the most difficult to handle.

A common cry of clergy spouses and children is that they feel 'second best' to the parish. The curate is always doing something for 'them', and seems to have less and less time and energy for the family. It can be particularly difficult when a curate is doing for parishioners precisely the sorts of things his own family are asking for (e.g. giving time to an elderly parishioner when her own mother needs a visit; playing football with the youth group whilst his own children are increasingly 'fitted in' to the gaps in his timetable). Indeed, relaxation together often gets squeezed out completely, and when the one who is ordained does take time off, all they seem to want to do is crash out in front of the television. Weekends become a thing of the past and Saturdays get taken over by weddings and parish events. Add to this the 'invasion' of the family home and privacy by the curate's study, telephone, fax, clutter, and even by the people of the parish, and resentment can build very quickly.

Jesus had some hard things to say about family relations, and he seemed to suggest that in the new dispensation of the kingdom, relationships with fellow believers are just as important as blood ties. Yet it is also clear from the Gospels that he took his family responsibilities seriously: his entrusting of his mother to John, the beloved disciple, at Calvary is a clear sign that care of family (whatever the pressures we may be under) is part of the calling of those who follow Christ. Curates may not always get the balance right, especially in the early days, but this is an area that clergy families need to revisit time and again as circumstances change and pressures ebb and flow.

Much of the latter half of this book aims to help curates deal with some of these practical pressures. Here, however, we are more concerned with the way in which the nature of family relationships may be affected by a curate's ordination.

God-like status or not?

> Aunt Mazelia was a devout Anglo-Catholic who was absolutely delighted that her nephew-in-law was now a priest; she had come up for the weekend to see the family and, more especially, to be present at Peter's second celebration of 'mass'. It was Saturday evening and Aunt Mazelia was going down with a cold . . . She sneezed rather explosively, and – without thinking, and simply to be polite – Peter said, 'Bless you!' Mazelia's face lit up and her heartfelt response was: 'Thank you, Peter – now, of course, you *can!*' Peter and his wife stifled their giggles, for Mazelia's words had been spoken in all sincerity – but they illustrated a memorable sense of shift in that particular relationship!

Like Peter, those who are ordained can sometimes be endowed with a strange god-like status by their family circle, suddenly becoming the 'fount of all wisdom' and focus of honour. On the other hand, a curate's nearest and dearest can often be those who keep his or her feet on the ground, reminding them just how fallible they are! Indeed, children (particularly teenagers) often seem to have a special gift for suppressing any illusions of holiness and superiority.

To be set on this sort of pedestal by members of the family can be hard to bear. To be reminded of one's frailty as a fallen human being – whilst uncomfortable – is undoubtedly healthy. Either way, it is important for curates to maintain some sort of 'reality check' with those to whom they are closest, so that relationships do not become distorted. Straight talking may sometimes be needed when unnecessary and unrealistic assumptions are being made about the role that a newly ordained member of the family should take. One way of dealing with such assumptions may be for a curate to be honest about his or her own needs and the pressures they are under, rather than pretending that their new status has somehow made them impervious to the everyday pressures of living in the twenty-first century. Another way is simply to keep holding up the needs of close family in prayer, for prayer has an uncanny way of defusing tricky situations and making clear our own part in creating them.

The clergy spouse

Ordination has a profound effect on marriage. Many adjustments may need to be made, and over the course of many years. Nevertheless, the way in which the recently ordained and their spouses work through the conflicts that may arise in the early days after ordination will frame the effectiveness with which they handle the pressures on their marriage in years to come. It is impossible to look at every aspect of the change in a marriage relationship at ordination here; instead, we will briefly explore just one that can bring into focus some of the stresses and pressures common to many: the particular demands on the spouse of a calling to non-stipendiary ministry.

For the spouse of a non-stipendiary minister, the physical upheaval of ordination may seem to be less: there may not be a house move, and much of life may seem to go on as before. Yet the 'inner shift', both for the spouse themselves and in the relationship between the spouse and the curate, can be immense. An OLM (and sometimes an NSM) will serve their title in the benefice that has nurtured them. At face value, this might seem to create a welcome continuity, but for a curate's spouse there can be difficulties in establishing new relationships with friends and fellow parishioners, particularly when their spouse is now perceived as being part of the 'inner circle'. In addition, it can be difficult for a curate's spouse in such a situation to know how to relate to their incumbent: after all, the incumbent is now the curate's boss, and it may no longer feel appropriate for the spouse to see him or her as their 'vicar', so the sense of loss may be doubled. At the other end of the spectrum is the situation where a curate is required to serve his or her title in a parish away from their home. Here again there will be loss and tension – perhaps a double loss – for the spouse, who has to choose where their loyalties lie: with the community or with their partner?

In most situations there needs to be some adjustment in the relationship between the clergy spouse and the incumbent once an NSM or OLM curate has been ordained, which can in turn affect the marriage relationship itself.

Edward had recently been ordained as curate at All Saints', where he was to serve as a non-stipendiary curate whilst continuing as deputy head of a large local primary school. He and his wife, Jo, were looking forward to getting involved in a new community and bringing their particular gifts and enthusiasms to parish life and worship. Jo was very musical and quickly became involved in the music group. Not long after she and Edward arrived, the leader of the music group moved away and the incumbent asked Jo to take over. She was delighted to have been asked, but some tensions and difficulties soon arose between her and Edward, and between each of them and the incumbent: Edward felt left out when Jo and the incumbent discussed things without him; the incumbent wrongly assumed that one partner would always pass messages on to the other; and Jo felt that Edward was crowding in on her all the time and couldn't ever allow her space to do her own thing.

Things to consider

Colleges and courses are able to give some recognition to the needs and concerns of spouses: the colleges still tend to have partners' groups, which can become a great source of support for the spouses of those in full-time training. Yet even here, learning can only be 'in anticipation': you cannot know what it's really like to be a clergy spouse until you experience it. Part-time courses and schemes have to work even harder to provide any sense of support or coherence for the spouses of those in training – and, clearly, many spouses (in both settings) would prefer not to be involved in their partner's training at all, and that wish must be respected.

It is questionable, however, whether the Church is able to offer support effectively even to those spouses of curates who would welcome it. Twenty years ago, when 'interest groups' of one sort or another were far more commonplace than they are today, the deanery clergy wives' group (sic) may have served as a place to share common concerns, frustrations and hopes. Things have changed, and such support networks are now comparatively rare, even if they were to be desired. With most clergy spouses now working (often to supplement family income), other mechanisms of support may be needed. One-to-one 'mentoring' from an experienced clergy spouse may be helpful, or peer group support for those whose partners have been recently ordained.

In the end, it is recognizing the need to maintain clear channels of communication that is at the heart of sustaining a clergy marriage: and communication – verbal and otherwise – takes time. If curates take their relationships with parishioners more seriously than their relationship with their spouse, then they are courting disaster – in the longer term at least. Taking days off together (including, if possible, the evening before a day off) and planning regular holidays away from phone and doorbell are vital. Without them, breakdowns of marriage and ministry are almost inevitable.

Relating to friends

Whether or not they are people of faith, many friends will be excited when a person announces that they are going to train for ordination. Others may fear that the person they have known will become 'holier-than-thou', distant and judgemental. There may be jokes about 'having to be good now', or suggestions about having a last good holiday before impecuniousness sets in. Often friends will simply be proud that someone they know is going to be a man or woman of the cloth.

Just as being ordained affects family relationships, so it can and does affect relationships with friends. Single curates will perhaps feel this most acutely, often feeling lonely and isolated in their new environment and desperate for people with whom to relax. They will need to work hard to establish new friendships in the new context. Yet will these really be friendships? Indeed, should they be? Will they be with people in the parish or those 'outside' – through leisure activities and so on? For such curates, pre-existing friendships may become especially important in the early days of a curacy: email messages may be frequent and mobile phone bills high!

Friends of a couple, friends of children and friends of a family as a whole can also be affected by the new status and role of the ordained person, and sometimes in ways that are unspoken and almost imperceptible. For a non-stipendiary curate who stays in or near their local community, the adjustment may be more subtle but no less demanding. How will their friendships with people at church be affected? Will they need to be more distant now that the curate is ordained and 'one of them' rather than 'one of us'? Or is it possible to set boundaries that allow pre-existing friendships to continue to flourish as if nothing has changed? We have seen already how difficult it can be for a spouse to handle these changes; the demands on friendships may be only slightly less taxing.

A test of friendship

Keeping friendships healthy is hard work. That is true for anybody, but it is, perhaps, especially true for those who are ordained. Lack of time, lack of energy, lack of weekends off – in short, lack of opportunity to nurture friendship in the way that it needs can mean that clergy can find themselves restricted to a circle of clergy colleagues and 'friends' who share their own experience. Cathedral cities are often awash with retired clergy who look to each other for friendship in retirement.

It is often in the early stages of ordained ministry that adjustments to friendships have to be made. Very occasionally, a friendship may have to come to an end. More often, ordination simply changes the dynamic of pre-existing friendships. For example, a curate and their spouse may need to learn a new independence, perhaps meeting another couple in twos rather than as a foursome on every occasion. Clearly, openness and honesty between partners is crucial if such relationships are to remain healthy.

Maintaining friendships

Jesus knew the value of friendship. He needed people close to him both physically and emotionally. He chose Peter, James and especially John to be there for him in his moments of greatest stress. He took time with them, and was careful to put relationships right when they had gone wrong (see John 21).

Relating to friends, like relating to family, is something that goes on whether a person is ordained or not. There is continuity: in almost every respect, the people involved are the same. They share a common history and experience; they probably share similar ideals and goals; they may have shared a good deal of themselves and their hopes and sorrows. Yet it is important to acknowledge that to be ordained can make a difference to such relationships, even if it is only in terms of the greater effort that may be required to sustain them. Just as with family relationships, there can be a temptation to take friendships for granted and not to invest in them the energy they need.

There is little in clergy training that addresses these sorts of issues for ordinands, and indeed, perhaps every person's way of handling these things will be different. It is important, however, that at some stage during their period of initial training curates are given the opportunity to reflect on such things with a supervisor, a spiritual director or a mentor. For it is one of the ways in which their 'being' may have changed.

Making friends in the parish

Making friends in the parish is often an area of concern for the newly ordained. There is a natural desire for the new curate (and his or her family) to want to become part of the community – to begin to belong. Sometimes, this is easier for the spouse and family (if there is one) than it is for the curate themselves, although it has to be said that those who move with young families will find themselves with 'friends' (courtesy of their offspring) whether they like it or not! The situation is very different for those who are single, for those without children, or for those whose own children have grown up and left home: the natural openings for creating new friendships are undoubtedly more limited.

Making friends in the parish, whilst it may be desirable, is not always helpful. There will be those in a parish who genuinely want to support the curate (and their family) through the ups and downs of their new job; there will be others, sadly, whose motives may be more mixed, and who would see the nurturing of friendship with the curate as a means of infiltrating and influencing parish strategy to their own ends. Discernment is always needed as friendships grow, but curates need to be particularly aware of these possibilities.

Often, matters of friendship become focused on the issue of how vulnerable a curate should or shouldn't be to members of the parish. Allowing others to recognize your need of help, prayer and support can be a way of deepening relationships and mutual trust; but it can also become an opening for gossip and manipulative behaviour. Curates, as much as anybody else, need the warmth of human contact and encouragement, but such friends need to be chosen carefully. For single curates, in particular, it may be important to have one or two people in the parish who can be there for you as 'you', and who are prepared to relate to you as a person rather than in role; but testing the boundaries of those friendships and the security of confidentiality is an important part of their development. As a general policy, it is wiser to be vulnerable to those who are well beyond the parish boundary, and who have no particular 'axes to grind' in relation to parish affairs. Building up such a network of support outside the parish is vital. Some curates agree to meet and pray with two or three others from their ordination peer group – from amongst those with whom they have trained at college or on a course. Such a clergy 'cell' (as it is sometimes known) can be a significant source of support in the early days of ministry – a safe place where support may be offered and the truth of a situation can be frankly told and heard.

Sometimes, however, the desire to make friends in the parish can be unrealistic. Many curates fall into the trap of hoping that their incumbent and his family will be 'friends'. Good working relationships with the incumbent and other church leaders are certainly important, but that does not necessarily mean that such people will be friends, and it may, in fact, be better if they are not! Here again we are confronted by the tension between 'personal' and 'professional': a training incumbent may be looking for a professional relationship with a colleague, while a curate may be looking for something more personal.

Another difficulty about making friends in the parish can be the way in which members of a church congregation or community interpret the relationship they have with the curate. Being a clergyperson requires 'small talk': the ability to make conversation and be (or at least appear to be) interested in the lives of those around. Such 'small talk' is often the foundation for deeper conversations of a more pastoral nature, and is a necessary (and usually helpful) element of the pastoral relationship. It can, however, be misinterpreted:

Mrs Upshaw was very upset one Christmas when she did not receive a card from the Reverend Miller, the parish's former curate who had left earlier that year. They had got on so well when he had been with them. She had written to him several times since he had left and although she knew he was busy, she hoped there would be some acknowledgement at Christmas. When she saw him at a parish celebration event the following spring, she made her disappointment known: 'I thought I would have heard from you,' she said. 'You were always so friendly towards me . . .'

Mrs Upshaw had summed up the situation in her own words: the Reverend Miller had been unswervingly 'friendly' – but that did not mean he was Mrs Upshaw's friend. Curates come and curates go, but lonely people can easily become attached to them and build up a fantasy about the nature of their relationship with them. It is something over which a curate can have little control, but an awareness of the danger is vital if further damage is to be avoided. A policy which many clergy find helpful is never to send Christmas cards to parishioners when they are in post: it avoids the danger of favouritism, as well as a significant expense! Adding a name to a Christmas list after leaving a parish can be a true indication of a friendship that has grown.[6]

Relating to secular work colleagues

One Wednesday afternoon in the summer, having tried to clear their desks of the most urgent matters, those who are to be ordained to a ministry in secular employment leave their office or workplace and head off for their pre-ordination retreat. The following Monday morning they are back again, to all appearances no different from when they went away. Are they in fact any different? And will people around them think they are, or treat them differently because there's now a 'Rev' at work? Compared to their stipendiary colleagues, who have probably moved to a different part of the country and begun to settle into a completely new community, their 'shift' in identity appears minimal; yet it is no less significant, and in some ways it is even more difficult to handle.

Reactions to the newly ordained will vary widely: there may be curiosity, ignorance, lack of interest; there may be a gentle condescension, such as that betrayed by the comment made to a newly ordained deacon: 'Good for you! I think everybody should have a hobby!' Whatever the reaction (or lack of it), the newly ordained may have a sense of being 'under the spotlight' – conscious that their every move, word and response may be being watched and noted to see whether they match up to the picture of perfection that might – unreasonably or not – be expected of one who is a 'Rev'. This is, of course, to exaggerate, but it points up the fact that, whereas a stipendiary curate is very quickly able to identify a role, or roles, within the life of the local church community, a minister in secular employment is not. Rarely is his or her ordination accompanied by the recognition of a specific 'place' or 'task' within the work context. Equally significant is the fact that, although they are probably aware of the preparation and training for ordained ministry that their employee has undergone, it is unlikely to be something the employer has requested or necessarily encouraged. The newly ordained employee is simply there, a given, an imposed and uninvited religious 'presence' within a work context that may have strict protocols concerning 'religious' activity within the workplace. For the newly ordained it can be a difficult and inwardly turbulent time: who they are may have changed, but their role as teacher, manager, accounts clerk, IT support person, farmer or whatever has not.

For many clergy in secular employment, there is a gradual process of learning to 'inhabit the role'. Whereas for the stipendiary curate there may be an emphasis on 'doing' – learning and perfecting new tasks and skills – for the deacon or priest in secular work there may be a greater emphasis on 'being'. To some extent it is a transition to being at ease with oneself as an ordained person, but it is also about beginning to recognize (often with some frustration) that 'being who you are' may (initially, at least) be the most significant element of your ministry to the work community. Often, this witness of integrity and faith will have been evident to colleagues with eyes to see for a long time before your ordination: it may speak with even greater intensity afterwards.

Most ministers in secular employment see intercession for their colleagues as a significant part of their calling. They may not have a designated 'sacred space' within which to pray, and yet all of their working environment may become for them a sacred space. Similarly, those who minister in secular employment often speak of the need to 'recognize the moment' when a more explicitly Christian ministry may be necessary or welcome.

A secondary school teacher who had recently been ordained found herself increasingly being asked to be a listening ear by colleagues. It was not always easy, for sometimes she would have to listen to the stories of colleagues who were at odds with each other, and she would have to remain impartial in her dealings with each. Over a period of time, however, she was able to foster reconciliation between disputing parties where previously a difference of opinion might have persisted.

Ministers in secular employment may not wear their collar 'on the outside', so to speak, but those around them may soon recognize them in their ordained capacity even without that outer identification. In fact, for some who are ordained it may feel very strange to put their clerical shirt and collar on at the end of the day in order to attend a 'church' meeting: in a very real (if unseen) sense, they have been ministering all day already.

It is clear that the adjustments required for ministers in secular employment are just as significant, if not more so, than for their stipendiary colleagues. It is therefore vital that within CME 1–4 programmes there is adequate provision for them to reflect upon their new ministries with peers and facilitators who understand their particular spheres of work and the demands that being ordained can make upon them. For too long, those who, because of their commitments, have been unable to fit into the patterns of ongoing support that have been set in place for stipendiary deacons and priests have simply been left to get on with things on their own. Spiritual directors, friends and peers can help to some degree, but more and more there is a need to provide 'tailored' CME for those whose primary sphere of ministry is their workplace, as well as giving them the opportunity to mix with their stipendiary colleagues. Not only do they need specialist support, but they have much to teach the wider ordained community about the 'being' of being a curate.

Relating to the wider community

The person coming new into a community enters with a 'clean slate', without history or prejudice, and may therefore be given the 'benefit of the doubt' for quite a significant period of time before judgements begin to be made about them and their effectiveness in ministry. An ordained person who lives and works in the community that has nurtured them – sometimes since childhood – brings with them both the riches of shared experience and history and the preconceptions of that community about the sort of person they are. Either way, ordination can affect expectations and the way in which relationships may continue to grow.

A number of factors need to be considered. First, there is the significance of residence. The traditional pattern of Anglican parochial ministry has emphasized both the necessity and the benefit of the ordained person living amongst the people he or she serves. In recent years, however, that model has been challenged, for both pragmatic and ideological reasons, as we have come to see that the resident, geographical community is no longer the sole (or, some would say, primary) locus of ministry. People belong to all sorts of different communities of work, leisure and interest, and move in and out of them frequently; for many, the place where they eat and sleep is simply that and nothing more.

Clearly, the Church does have to continue to think creatively about patterns of ministry, but in many rural areas the traditional pattern (or at least the idea of the traditional pattern) prevails. In spite of the changing culture, residence continues to be a factor in how communities relate to their ordained clergy. Most stipendiary curates will live in the parish or benefice they serve. For ordained local ministers, this is a prerequisite of their selection and an assumed dimension of their future ministry. Increasingly, however, non-stipendiary curates are being deployed in parishes and benefices at some distance from their place of residence, in a community that may be geographically adjacent but is in every other respect removed from the one they have known hitherto, and in which they have been known. Such curates may fall between two stools: they are neither 'new' yet resident, nor are they 'known' yet resident. Instead they are 'unknown' and not resident.

Without detracting from the benefits and, indeed, the necessity of a deployable non-stipendiary ministry, the challenges presented by this scenario may be considerable. Aside from the costs, in time, energy and expenses, of commuting to a more distant benefice, it may prove impossible for a non-stipendiary minister's family to participate in the life of the church and community where he or she operates. This can simply add to the pressures already experienced by the family of the newly ordained. It can also lead to a conflict of interest and expectations between the community of residence and that of ministry or service: which has priority when the summer fete of both falls on the same day? As the traditional pattern of 'one priest one parish' continues to break down, further reflection needs to be undertaken on the significance (or not) of residence and its effect, for good or ill, on the life of both the ordained and their families and on the community(ies) they seek to serve.

A second factor in how a newly ordained person relates to the wider community concerns the assumptions that may be made (on both sides) where there are pre-existing relationships, particularly when a curate's personal circumstances change. Sadly, there is sometimes a breakdown in a marriage relationship or some significant bereavement that may render a person's ministry more limited for a period of time. Whilst it is not always helpful or appropriate for the detail of such circumstances to be made public, a community inevitably becomes aware of the fact that 'something' is wrong. However, such change in normal patterns may come about for entirely joyful reasons – the curate's pregnancy, for example! Whether she is stipendiary or not, such personal circumstances will – at some point – become visible to all, and even this can bring about inappropriate expectations(!) and assumptions.

Carol's baby was due in about four months. Although it was her second child, she thought it might be helpful to catch up on the latest developments in childbirth wisdom and baby care, and so she subscribed to a chat room of other mums who were expecting children at about the same time as Carol. She remained 'just a mum' for several weeks until eventually the chat room conversation got around to asking the question 'What do you do for a living?' Carol hesitated, but decided in the end to admit to being a priest. All carried on as usual until the point at which one of the chat room mums gave birth prematurely; her baby was in intensive care, and a request was posted via the chat room for Carol to pray for the newborn child. This she was more than happy to do, but what came with it was a significant shift in her relationship with the other chat room mums: Carol was now a priest, whereas before she had been just another mum.

After Carol's baby was born, she took her statutory maternity leave before gradually moving back into full-time ministry. She found it fascinating to hear the comments, first, of those who had assumed that she would not be coming back to work full time 'because she will want to be with the children', and second, of those who assumed not only that she would be coming back to work full-time, but that she would no doubt now be running the mother and toddler group to which her own two children were taken by the child-minder. Neither set of assumptions was correct!

Third, becoming a public figure in the community can both increase and limit boundaries for communication. For example, whereas before ordination a person may have felt at liberty to support a particular view in village politics, it may no longer be helpful to do so: a certain neutrality may be required. On the other hand, it may become even more difficult to speak with a prophetic voice into a community where one is already known: 'A prophet is not without honour . . .' Jesus himself discovered this when he preached in the synagogue at Nazareth (Luke 4.16ff.).

Without wishing to undo the foundation of a relationship that already exists with a community, it is important that those who are ordained, and so become public figures in the community, are helped to reflect on whether it might be appropriate to establish new patterns of relating, and to set new boundaries and ways of communicating with those who have known them over many years. That this will happen naturally and easily cannot be taken for granted. Some curates will take to the public role more easily than others; some will find it easier in a community that already knows them; others will find this extraordinarily hard. Again, what matters is that there is a safe place where curates can reflect on those changes and be helped to deal with them – both for their own sake, and for that of their families and friends who may become caught up in the transition.

It has become clear that ordination can have a significant effect on who we think we are, on how we relate to others, and on how others relate to us. None of these things is tangible before ordination, and it is difficult to envisage how training institutions might prepare ordinands and their families for the impact ordination may have. What matters is that there are support structures in place within a diocese, or through other networks – personal or structural – to help the newly ordained to adjust to new ways of perceiving themselves and of being perceived by others. This is crucial if they are to continue to follow their vocation to be and to become the person God is calling.

3 'He who calls you is faithful': continuity of vocation

The period between a person's first acknowledgement that they think they may be being called to ordained ministry and the time when they are in their first curacy is one of considerable change and development. They will have been through a process of discernment, both local and national; they will have become part of a community of training, full- or part-time; and they will have had to handle the myriad of feelings and practical demands that that brings, including, amongst others:

- a possible dislocation of place (perhaps for ordinand and family), and the need to establish new relationships with tutors and peer group;

- dealing with new concepts in theology, new experiences in practice and challenges to understandings of self, others and God;

- a possible sense of their previous life experience being undervalued, and the deskilling that often comes with learning a completely new subject and new skills.

By the time they come to the end of their training, ordinands are, in some ways at least, 'different' people from those they were only two or three years previously.

Yet the sense of shifting identity doesn't stop there. Relationships change; the newly ordained have to begin to learn to work in a new, much more public role than they may have had previously; and they will find themselves answerable to an incumbent and an institution in a way that may be quite alien to their previous working environment. Even within a curacy, the sequence of changing identities continues as a deacon becomes a priest, with all the internal and external 'shift' that accompanies that transition. It is small wonder that curates can find themselves wondering who they really are.

For many curates, it is their ordination to the priesthood that 'seals' their awareness of God's faithfulness to them over a journey that has possibly taken many years. Not that being ordained priest is an end in itself; rather, it is a significant marker in the continuing unfolding of a person's response to God's call to become who they fully are.

Ordination to the diaconate is often accompanied (as we have seen) by significant change, both external and internal; yet for many deacons, the tasks of ministry can feel more like a continuation of what they have already done as a lay person and as an ordinand. By contrast, ordination to the priesthood can feel like something of a paradigm shift: the priest is set apart by the community of believers to be and to act in a particular way on behalf of that community, and to serve it as pastor and minister of the sacrament as well as minister of the word. Recent theological study has opened up our understanding of diaconal ministry as world-facing and world-focused — a servant ministry, yes, but one that is primarily acting as an agent of service between the gathered community of the faithful and the wider community within which it is set.[7] The ministry of the priest, however, whilst still encompassing that of the deacon, is primarily to serve the gathered people of God as they exercise their corporate priesthood within and towards the world. As such, it demands a shift of emphasis and a shift in thinking as well as practice.

Deacons are often poorly prepared for their ordination to the priesthood, such preparation being limited to a session on 'how to preside at the Eucharist' rather than being seen as an opportunity to think through and reflect upon the quite different ministry into which they are moving. The practical changes are important without doubt, but so are the internal ones. So what is it that keeps curates going through all this change? What is the thread that reassures them that they are not going to go completely 'off the rails' and that there is some sense and continuity about this whirlwind of a journey? The answer is trust in the faithfulness of God's call.

The one upon whom the bishop lays hands at deaconing or priesting is the same person who first spoke to their spouse or their vicar several years earlier about the possibility of being ordained: and yet they are different. They have changed: they have gone through a period of formation into the mind and likeness of Christ that is the calling of every disciple, and they will continue to change as they serve him in the ordained ministry.

Yet it is important to recognize that, just as we change and develop as persons over the years, so our vocation changes and develops too: as those whom God has called, we are asked both to be and to become. In other words, we are (or should be) constantly growing into our vocation as disciples of Jesus Christ. As Archbishop Rowan Williams has put it:

> Vocation doesn't happen, once and for all, at a fixed date. Paul himself, who seems to be the classic instance to the contrary, recognises this precisely in talking about being set apart from his mother's womb. It happens from birth to death; and what we usually call vocation is only a name for the moment of crisis within the unbroken process.[8]

So there is both continuity and change — and those two elements are both present in what is perhaps the most significant moment of your whole curacy: when you are ordained priest. You are still the curate; you are still you; yet your ministry takes on a new and richer and deeper dimension when, by the laying on of hands and the invocation of the Holy Spirit, you become a priest. At this point perceptions change again and the 'being' of being a curate is further transformed. There will be those who will want to build you up into someone special and great because you are now a priest: the truth is you become ever more aware of your smallness and dependence on God.

The central relationship

So far in this chapter, we have focused on changes in the perception of self, and have recognized that who we are and understand ourselves to be is shaped and framed by the relationships we have with others. Important as these relationships are, however, it is our relationship with God that matters most: it too must be reflected upon, moulded and reshaped as we grow and change. A curate's relationship with God needs to be given just as much care and attention as their relationships with others. For how may we expect truly to be and to become those whom God is calling unless we work on our relationship with him as part of the process? Perhaps this is stating the obvious – yet perhaps the obvious needs to be stated. For the sheer busyness of those who have been recently ordained can prevent time for prayer, study and reflection on God's word.

Communication is essential if relationships are to grow; and as we communicate we become who we are, in both our human relationships and in our relationship with God. In a very real sense, we become who we are in conversation with him. Whatever stage we are at in the process of thinking about or being an ordained minister, vocation (including, but not limited to, vocation to ordained ministry) is about response to the God who calls us into being and calls us by name. It is not about 'doing a job'; it is, as Rowan Williams goes on to suggest, 'about saving your soul':

> It has to do with recognising that my relation with God (and so with everybody) depends absolutely on making the decision to be what I am, to answer God's Word ... because what I am is already known and loved and accepted in God.[9]

This relationship of call and response lies at the heart of all vocation, and must lie at the heart of a curate's relationship with the God they serve. It is this communication with God that gives life to personhood as a disciple of Jesus Christ and as an ordained disciple in particular.

So often prayer, meditation, time spent with God in silent reflection on his word, his world and his people becomes crowded out by the demands of the role: 'I cannot stop, I cannot pray, I cannot go away on retreat – because somebody needs me ... ' Yet who is the 'me' they need? Is it the person you once were, or the person you think you ought to be? Is it the model curate – the one for whom the Church has been waiting for so long? Or is it the 'you' you really are? Who is it God has called, and is still calling?

These sorts of questions can only be pondered in the company of trusted friends, a spiritual director and God himself. None of us can discover the truth of who we are in isolation. We have to go on asking, 'Who do people say that I am?';

and we have to go on listening to those who will tell us gently and truthfully who it is they see and hear. Ultimately, we have to be willing to kneel before God in our nakedness and give him time to respond to our question as well . . .

'Being a curate' is, for many, an idea that eventually becomes a reality. The role that was once just a dream is now being lived. Yet one of the dangers of being a curate is that in taking on the role, you can somehow lose the person inside. You do all the right things and fulfil all the expectations, but, like the ordinand on the night before her priesting, you suddenly discover that the person you thought you were has gone missing, and something or someone else has taken their place.

Keeping God at the centre is one of the most demanding things about being a curate. Perhaps that seems strange when so much of a curate's time is spent leading others in worship and being a 'professional pray-er'. Yet it is true. In this regard, it is vital to ensure that there is a distinctive place and time for personal prayer, over and above the place and time for public worship; this may be in a different chapel within the church building, or in the study at home, or in the car, or on a regular walk. It may be as part of, or alongside the saying of the daily offices, in church or at home, but what matters is that there is a personal 'tuning in' to the voice of God each day, as well as a professional 'tuning in' on behalf of others. We have to be and become pray-ers too, beyond the role.

God is not interested in roles, but in people. God does not call us to play a part, but to become who we are. Reflection on the 'being' of being a curate is one of the ways in which we can get beneath the role to discover the relationships that matter – with family, friends, colleagues, the community, and above all with our faithful God himself. It is then that we may serve him most fully. It is then that we are most fully ourselves.

5

Public ministry

John Witcombe

It may come as a surprise to ordinands and their families that ordination does not confer miraculous transformation of the character. Nor should it: it is the person who has been chosen and ordained for service, not some cardboard cut-out. We bring to ministry all that we are – our history, our experiences, our successes and our failures. As the previous chapter demonstrated, we bring ourselves into every ministerial situation: as we see in the next chapter, the supervision relationship should help us recognize the impact this makes, for good or ill, both on the ministry and upon ourselves.

Personal or professional?

What does a minister bring to each pastoral encounter? Perhaps a diagram will help to identify this:

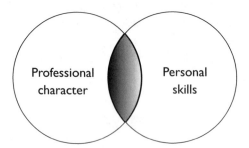

Ministers bring the professional skills from training and experience that enable them to fulfil the expectations of the parishioners – expectations of competence and ethical behaviour, for example. They also bring their own character – their personality, their human experience. On some occasions, professional skills will be simply inadequate, and all that can be offered, for example to a bereaved mother, is personal identity with a suffering person sharing a common humanity. On other occasions, professional skills are exceptionally important – at a funeral, perhaps.

There can also be times when our personal character and history may threaten to disable our professionalism: an unexpected encounter may trigger unresolved issues from our past, and the ministry becomes an occasion for meeting our own needs. On the other hand, it is possible for professionalism so to mask human identity that an individual's ministry becomes soulless.

The hope is that a minister will work within the hatched area of the diagram, bringing both their own unique personality and their professional competence to each situation. This means that each pattern of ministry will be unique.

I had my own experience of this most powerfully soon after the death of someone very close to me. Only a few weeks later, another family member, my great-aunt, who had been equally full of life and pink gin, and memorably present at my wedding, died – and I was asked to take the funeral. I knew that I could only do this by separating out my own raw experience of bereavement and 'going professional' in the worst sense of the word, excluding the whole of my 'personal' circle from my ministry in that context. My grief was so powerful and unresolved at that time that it would have disabled my professional responsibility to have primary concern for the other mourners in the funeral. This was not why I had been asked to take the service, so I said that I would rather not. Some years later, I was asked to officiate at the funeral of another aunt, whom I also knew well and who was an equally memorable character. On this occasion, having moved through my own resolution of grief, I was able to bring my personal experience of both bereavement and my aunt together with my professional competence to offer a service that was uniquely appropriate for the family at the time.

When asked what they are looking for in Christians, and especially in ministers, many enquirers will respond with the single word 'integrity'. It can be difficult, though, to learn how to be both properly professional and at the same time true to oneself when exercising public ministry. Other chapters of this book explore some of the complexities of this area. In this chapter, I would like to consider the manner or style of public ministry, and how each minister may develop a style that appropriately reflects their experience of God and their unique character and vocation.

The parish in which a curate serves will have its own expectations, as will the supervising incumbent. In the early weeks and months of ministry, the curate may well be encouraged simply to 'fit in' – to follow what is familiar to the people in that place. As time goes on, they will begin to find their own voice, their own way of making the gospel present to those to whom they are ministering. This is not necessarily easy, but it is the way to maturity in the Christian community.

Leading worship

Leading worship is a performance. That is not to say it has no integrity, but rather that it is a way of drawing others into a reality that is communicated by the worship leader's words and actions. The leader performs the words and actions that express the heart of the Christian tradition, inviting the congregation to make them their own. This is the nature of public ministry: what the leader does in church, or other areas of their Christian life, is no longer individual, private. It has a symbolic character: it is there to enable others to identify the worship that is already present in their own lives, and to open up new ways of expressing themselves in relationship to God.

It seems obvious that a worship leader should mean what they say. The integrity in the life of the leader will be its own symbol, and will draw forth a response from those in the church and community. Integrity alone is, however, not enough: there must also be the ability to project and 'take the stage'. This can feel artificial to new worship leaders: surely I'm not 'being myself'? The answer is probably to say: you are being yourself – but more so! I once heard the actor-priest who played the part of the vicar in *Dad's Army* being asked to comment on the assertion that 'vicars are just failed actors'. His response was penetrating: 'Not *too* failed, I hope.'

There is nothing wrong in being self-deprecating. To be so in public ministry, however, will be to fail those we have been asked to lead. This is not to say that we should be so hale and hearty that we browbeat the suffering souls in the congregation with cheery good mornings and calls to 'do it again with feeling'. Speaking personally, isn't it extraordinary that we do not have directors for church services, just as even the most accomplished actors rely on others to enable them to draw the most from the material they have to present.

All of this may suggest that the minister's own worshipping needs are irrelevant to their public ministry. This is not true – but their responsibility extends beyond their own needs to those of the whole congregation. A newly ordained curate became so caught up in the beautiful choir anthem that he quite lost track of the administration of communion in which he was engaged: this may be inspiring to others as an isolated incident, but a reoccurrence would not be welcome.

Collaborative ministry, and good preparation, can make it easier for ministers to focus upon their own relationship with God during a service so that the flow of the service is not disturbed.

Liturgical texts: scaffolding or straitjacket?

To lead Anglican worship is to use liturgical texts. These texts have become symbols for many in our congregations, carrying a weight (some would say freight) of meaning that far outweighs a single recitation, but which echoes and is enhanced in each retelling. Presenting them well is a serious duty: changing words here and there, or omitting large sections, may be justified on occasion to enable the juxtaposition of familiar and unfamiliar to awaken new layers of meaning, but as a general rule, it does violence to our congregations to depart from the texts that have served as reliable guides to a place of opening our lives to God, and his life to us, for many years. The texts also serve as a safety line in turbulent waters, or a guide rope in the dark, at times when our own faith seems inadequate to the very public task to which we've been called. The minister may well find herself asking 'Can I say this today?' – yet, in saying it, discover that the Spirit awakens meaning within her, as she is after all able to lay her life before a God who holds her in his love.

There are good reasons for departing from the standard texts from time to time: new developments in the understanding of both church and worship embodied in the *Mission-shaped Church* report, and the provisions of *Common Worship*, encourage creativity and innovation. This is excellent, although the dangers of 'change for change's sake', and self-indulgence on the part of service leaders, are real. Good resources are available for guiding creative liturgical development which may most usefully be considered collaboratively. However, I would suggest that the wide range of alternative forms of worship should remain for the present as just that: alternative. They depend for their value on the existence of a recognized 'standard form', and should not replace it entirely.

Finding your own style

Even the briefest of reflections will reveal a huge diversity in the ways that we have seen others lead worship. It may not be obvious to us, but we, too, will develop our own style in leading – a style which will be helpful to some and not to others. A newly ordained curate may be trained by their receiving incumbent to follow the incumbent's style: sometimes this can extend to peculiar mannerisms to which the vicar is quite oblivious!

Style in leading is a concrete expression of the principle of uniting the personal and the professional in ministry. Most congregations do not want to see 'someone different' in the pulpit or at the altar from the person they talk to before or after the service. It is true that the mere act of leading worship and preaching may at first seem so unusual, so alien, in spite of the training, that it is hard to find a way of 'being yourself'. Nevertheless, it is appropriate to aim to find a way of being in public ministry that is true to the role, to the appropriate expectations of the congregation, and to your personal characteristics.

A way of doing this is for the newly ordained minister consciously to look for those who may offer a model of being in ministry for them to follow. The American preacher David Schlafer has helpfully described the concept of 'preaching parents': those who have influenced us and whom we either react against or seek to emulate.[1] The concept may apply to all forms of ministry. If we have experienced a very 'laid-back' style, for example, we may ourselves have either adopted such a manner, or reacted against it. If a curate finds herself uncomfortable with the style of leadership modelled in the church, but cannot find a style that enables her to be herself in the role, she may find it helpful to visit other churches, or carefully watch others lead at diocesan or other events.

Style is a matter of theology as well as of personality – although it is a 'chicken and egg' argument as to which comes first. Does a conservative, authoritarian theology lead to or emerge from a particular personality type? It will be true that what we are communicates as loudly – perhaps even more so – than what we say, and the theology of our lives, the way in which we relate to God, will show itself to the congregation whether or not we preach it. It's probably best to recognize this and seek to offer a theology that is clearly congruent with the life that they see.

Leading Holy Communion

Some colleges and courses train their students in the practicalities of presiding at Holy Communion. This is one of the areas of ministry in which churchmanship, or theological tradition, is most in evidence. For this reason there may be little sense in seeking to prepare too much before moving into a parish, as the style of a curate's presidency will almost certainly need to follow existing parish practice.

The manner of presiding – whether to genuflect or elevate the sacrament, even whether or not to robe – may not be in any way under the curate's control. This can be enriching, but it can also be exceptionally frustrating and even disorientating as familiar signposts to the role and the significance of the event are either changed or removed altogether. It is important for the newly ordained to have, maintain and develop their own personal understanding of what they are doing, and why they are doing it.

A curate presiding at communion in a context that has more ritual acts than they are used to should work hard both to understand the incumbent's and the congregation's understanding of these acts (they may well discover there is little beyond 'we've always done it this way') and to discover their own. What does it mean to kiss the altar, for example? – with its origins in the devotion to relics kept in any genuine altar, it may seem an empty and unhelpful ritual today. However, as a mark of acknowledgement and reverence for the place where Christ makes himself present for us today in the sacrament, it may be a worthwhile expression of prayer.

It can be just as hard for a curate who is deprived of some of his customary marks of recognition of God's presence in the rite: it can feel simply rude to fail to genuflect in the presence of the sacrament, for example. This may be a matter to explore with the help of a spiritual director, but the spirituality of reverence for Christ giving himself to us in the sacrament should not be made dependent upon outward signs. It is possible, for example, for the priest to preside wearing 'invisible robes': the self-identity and dignity that robes signify can be taken into the most informal of contexts in the consciousness of the president.

In each of these situations, good communication between vicar and curate is essential. It can be healthy for a church to observe diversity in devotional practice between those in leadership, as long as they are clearly content to allow the other space to be themselves before God. It may be that you can agree to lead in different ways, taking care, of course, to avoid a congregational division following either party. In very many churches there is little teaching on 'why we do what we do': such education will help avoid any sense of division. A willingness to ask either obvious or difficult questions on the part of the curate may open up new opportunities for understanding and spiritual renewal throughout a church – not necessarily by changing the way things are done, but by facilitating a greater engagement with their significance.

Preaching

Preaching is either a joy or a nightmare for many of those new to ordained ministry. It will be some years before it becomes routine. All those ordained will have had significant attention given to this ministry in their training, and it is therefore not necessary to revisit the basics here.[2]

The development of a style in preaching is not simply an individual affair. Just as traditional BBC microphones used to pick up from both sides – one side for the speaker, and one for the audience – so the development of a preaching style should be a reflection of the relationship between the curate and the church. There will be large services and small services, occasions when one approach or another is called for, and opportunities should be offered and taken to develop skills in a variety of situations. It will often be appropriate to preach from brief notes, freeing the speaker to engage with the congregation – but there will also be occasions that call for the careful weighing of each word, and hence require the use of a meticulously prepared full script.

Those approaching ordination frequently wonder how they will be resourced for their preaching: how will they keep finding things to say? The various preaching handbooks are a useful guide to potential resources. Mark Greene, of the London Institute of Contemporary Christianity, has written helpfully of the importance of listening to God, Scripture and the world, and of the necessity of staying in touch with the questions and life situations of the congregation.[3] It may not be possible to participate regularly in a church home group, but it remains true that conversations in home groups, or enquirers' groups, as well as other pastoral visits, are often the catalysts for the best sermons.

If possible, gather a small group together who will offer feedback on your preaching and other aspects of your public ministry. Just as actors need directors, so ministers need help in developing their gifts to ensure that they are getting the message across, and genuinely helping others meet with God. It's not enough to leave it to chance.

Occasional offices

This rather peculiar name refers to baptisms, weddings and funerals – services (or 'offices') held as the occasion demands. They are a time-consuming and draining, but often deeply rewarding, part of parish ministry. They are also curiously separate, for the most part, from the job of building up the life of the congregation.

In each of these offices, the ordained person has a particular role as the 'host', enabling those present to engage with one another, with God and, importantly, with themselves – their emotions, their beliefs, their response to the rite of passage in which they are caught up. It is an area where many curates will feel ill prepared and out of their depth, perhaps swamped by the human need that surrounds them, but where many will also feel particularly conscious of being equipped by God for the role.

It is well recognized that the occasional offices represent the Church's part in the stages of transition that belong to society as a whole. It is good for ministers to both recognize and respect this, not attempting to wrest control inappropriately, but instead gratefully accepting the opportunity that our culture offers to weave Christian meaning into the identity changes that the rites embody. A significant part of this, of course, is to be welcoming of those involved: this means, at least, smiles, eye contact, and getting the names right. All else is secondary. In the brief notes that follow, many of the principles are transferable from one occasion to another.

Baptisms

Churches have widely varying baptism policies which generally reflect their theological basis. Some will offer baptism freely to all who ask, others will encourage alternatives for those who are not part of the worshipping community. It can be hard for a curate to find themselves in a parish whose approach does not easily chime with their own – and this is an area of 'conscientious objection' for some, from either perspective.

The balance between 'pastoral' and 'theological' integrity may seem more difficult to maintain in baptism than in the other offices. In fact, baptismal practice usually makes sense against its church context: those in a sacramentally based church which offers baptism to any who ask will not usually struggle to find a grace-filled efficacy in the rite, whereas members of a more proclamatory model will naturally move towards a less general invitation. A curate will probably do well to fit in with the practice of the local fellowship, learning through embodying their theology even if it is not immediately congenial.

Baptism services are, like the other occasional offices, opportunities to express the commitment of God to us throughout our lives – to express joy at new birth, and the ultimate hope of those united to Christ in baptism. It is, of course, a place to challenge those present to commitment – but not to try to put words into people's mouths that they cannot say with integrity. It is a place to encourage the whole church community to express their support and welcome for those who choose to come to God at this special moment in their lives.

Weddings

Weddings give the opportunity for a curate to shine! The bride and groom, to say nothing of their family and friends, are usually full of joy and anxiety in equal measure, and need the minister's help to enable them to relax enough during the ceremony to be themselves, and to engage with the awesome reality of the commitment they are making. Like that of Jesus at the wedding in Cana, the curate's presence may initially be a source of confusion or embarrassment, but in the end it can be the transforming touch that brings God's love alive.

Preparation is vital: in the rehearsal, there will be an opportunity for the officiating minister to form a personal relationship with the couple, to facilitate the encouraging glances that will help them through the service a day or two later. Gathering information about immediate family and friends will enable appropriate words of welcome to be spoken, and any special arrangements made for the seating. The accurate filling in of wedding registers will be a source of greater anxiety to many ministers than the liturgy. A piece of paper placed in the service book with the full names of the couple written clearly on it in capitals can be a useful aide-memoir if you are afraid of forgetting the names halfway through the ceremony.

In a wedding service, the minister has one eye on the couple and one on the gathered congregation: the service exists for both, as both play a part in the commitment to the new partnership, the new life that is being established. It's a time for celebration – and the minister may be wanted on the photographs!

Funerals

More than anything else, both funeral visit and service are occasions when ministers will feel unsure of their own abilities. Yet whether you are walking up a garden path to knock on a strange door, sitting amidst the tears of family and friends, walking in front of a coffin or standing at a crematorium chapel lectern, these are the times when vocation comes to the fore: I am only here, says the curate, because God has called me, and I can rely on him for what these people need.

It's not possible to sum up a person's life in a few minutes. It is possible, though, to reflect back to the grieving family some of their own memories, to enable the one who has died to become present to them again in the service as they are commended into God's care. The theology of the funeral liturgy is clear: we are to hold up the love and hope of God, expressed in the person of Jesus Christ, as a promise, invitation and challenge to all who are present.

Funerals are, paradoxically, one of the most satisfying areas of ministry for many clergy. Taking a funeral service can feel very close to the reason that someone was ordained: to witness to God's love in a hard place. It is both beyond, and yet achievable within, human ability – with God's help. The following notes set out one model of how to approach the ministry of funerals. It isn't the only way – but it may help you work out your own approach. I have included considerably more detail about this ministry than other occasional offices because experience demonstrates that many of the greatest anxieties about beginning public ministry arise in the context of funerals – and curates may often find themselves handling such ministry very soon after their ordination, without the accompanying guidance of their incumbent, who is enjoying a well-earned summer break!

As with weddings, careful preparation is of the utmost importance. There are far too many people whose one contact with the institutional Church has been 'the vicar who got Dad's name wrong'.

At the visit

I establish the facts about:

- the name of the deceased – what were they actually called?;

- family relationships

- particular friends (who may feel the loss most)

- working life

- hobbies and ways of spending their leisure time – where did they go on holiday?

- if the deceased was one part of a couple, I often ask how they met, and find out some history

- what are the surviving partner's particular memories?

- evidence of faith ('Did he have much to do with church . . .?').

I inform them of:

- the purpose of the funeral – to face up to what's happened in the context of Christian hope

- the length of the service (they often say 'We don't want it too long').

I ask them about hymns, readings (sometimes), anything else they'd like said.

We usually laugh quite a lot, I usually pray (they usually cry), and I often have a cup of tea.

By the end, we usually know that we get on very well (even if I look rather young for a minister).

At the crematorium

I arrive ten minutes early;

I put my books ready on the lectern and I pray in the chapel;

I chat to the organist;

I check where the button is to close the curtains;

I wait outside for the cars;

I greet the family, and get introduced to any I haven't met.

I have the service written out on a piece of A4 folded in half, with:

- The name (including 'known as') in large block letters at the top of the sheet

- Sentences (I read from the book – and I have crossed out the ones I don't find helpful)

- Prayer (sometimes)

- Either first hymn, or Psalm 23

- Address

- Bible reading (usually John 14)

- Prayers (selected from book, and including the Lord's Prayer)

- Commendation

- Hymn (if applicable)

- Psalm 103 (or 121)

- Committal (selective sentences from book)

- Closing prayer

- Blessing.

I then write out the address. I do this every time, even though the detail will only vary in particular respects, because it helps to fix it in my mind before the service:

- What we're here for – to celebrate the life of N., and to share grief.

- We're all in shock – death is a shock, and we need each other's support.

- Share memories as a way of support – treasure your best memories.   Each of you have special memories of N. – whether __ __ as a [wife, mother, friend, colleague, neighbour, etc.] – of [happy times in the caravan at Ingoldmells . . . digging the garden . . . ballroom dancing . . . at the shoe factory . . .].

- Life for N. was [tough, easy, joyful, sad . . .] but God was with [him, her] . . .

- God offers his love to us throughout our lives and at the end of them, inviting us to turn to him and put our trust in him ... Jesus died to show that nothing (not even death) is stronger than the love of God ... his resurrection shows that nothing is stronger than the hope of God ... we turn to God in this service, through Jesus Christ (usually move to John 14 for reading).

It may not matter so much what you say as the way you say it. Lots of eye contact and smiling will help! Often, you can draw from what the family have told you to make the congregation laugh – that always helps.

I turn to face the coffin for the words of committal – it helps to focus the congregation's attention on the important thing that's about to happen. I discourage mourners from leaving the curtains open – I think the visual sign of separation is important. After the blessing I shut my eyes and pray whilst waiting for the funeral director to come in. If he takes too long, I sometimes go up to the family and speak to them for a moment.

As they leave at the end of the service, I greet everyone with a handshake and a word of farewell.

At the cemetery

Much of the above applies in the same way until after the commendation and the hymn, beginning in the chapel at the cemetery. You then need to move out of the chapel to the graveside. Usually, you will walk beside the funeral director in front of the hearse. If it's a long way, you'll get taken in the car. If it's raining, you may want to wear a cloak or have someone hold an umbrella.

When you arrive by the grave, walk ahead of the family and go to stand at the head of the grave. Make sure your footing is secure! As the mourners begin to gather round, the undertakers will take the straps under the coffin and look to you for the nod to begin to lower the coffin into the grave (usually accompanied with a brisk 'Thank you, gentlemen' from the funeral director). Before I give this nod, and as the family gather, I read something – usually Psalm 121 (it seems to suit the open air). I give the nod to lower the coffin as I am reading the psalm.

Once they are gathered, I read something else – usually Psalm 103 – and I may say a prayer, partly to give people time to adjust to being there, because the ceremony itself is very short at this stage. I then move through the committal in the normal way. The funeral director will often throw a handful of earth on the coffin at the words 'earth to earth' – or sometimes the family will do this. After the blessing I may invite the family to draw nearer to look in, and then I move away towards the path, where the flowers will have been laid, and wait to say goodbye to the mourners.

A service in church

Large funerals, and funerals of church members are likely to take place in the church. Special care needs to be given to the family, for whom this can make it a very drawn-out occasion, especially if there is a long journey on to the cemetery or crematorium. Care may also be needed to develop the liturgical and musical content of the service to make it appropriate for the church setting: liturgy which is appropriate for the crematorium chapel may not suit another environment.

In church, you need to be aware of where the coffin will be, and position yourself on the correct side of it to speak to the family (don't end up peering through a mass of flowers). You may well find that a family member or friend wants to give a tribute or eulogy – try to get a script, or at least talk to them first if you can, to help ensure it's appropriate. Also be aware that they may not be able to finish because they may be overcome with emotion.

At the end of a church service, I usually read the Nunc dimittis as I walk back down the aisle in front of the coffin. At the door, I may end up greeting people, but I usually try to avoid doing this, so that we can move on as smoothly as possible to the crematorium or graveyard. (Not many of you will have an 'active' graveyard by the church.)

At the cemetery or crematorium, I simply carry on from the appropriate place in the service, usually using Psalm 121 to go into the chapel at the crematorium, or following the same order for burials as described above.

In churches of a more Catholic tradition, you may be asked to receive the coffin into church the night before – there are good prayers for this in the new *Common Worship* liturgy. You may also be asked to hold a funeral service in the context of Holy Communion – local practice varies very widely on this.

Pastoral visiting

I was once told that an indispensable characteristic for a priest was an 'insatiable curiosity for what goes on behind your parishioners' front doors'. Genuine interest in other people, in their lives and joys and sorrows and in the place of God within those, comes naturally to many who are ordained. It is also the bedrock of all parish work: why preach if you are not interested in those to whom you are preaching?

Styles of visiting, however, vary enormously. For one priest, an ideal afternoon's visiting is where most parishioners are out, and duty is fulfilled by posting a visiting card through the letterbox. Others thrive on personal contact. Visiting at different times of day will take quite different forms: afternoon visits can tend to be more relaxed, less focused, and longer than morning visits. Evening visits can feel invasive of people's relaxation time, and may need to have a clear purpose – one that is strong enough to withstand the competition from the television that you will encounter in many households.

At the heart of all visiting is the desire to establish relationships and explore contexts, break down isolation and broaden vision – for both priest and people – of the many ways in which God is discovered in our midst. Listening skills are essential for visiting ministers, both to others and to God. Other practical questions and skills are also necessary: should the minister pray, for example, and if so, how? Prayer, strangely, can seem more embarrassing for the minister anxious not to impose than for the parishioner, who is probably expecting it – and perhaps hoping for it. A short, simple, informal prayer, perhaps followed by the Lord's Prayer, is often most appropriate. One other indispensable skill is leaving: bringing conversations to a natural conclusion takes a lifetime to master, and even then a minister may sometimes be reduced to fighting their way past a reluctant individual, even driving away as the parishioner continues to talk.

Hearing confessions

The sacrament of reconciliation is one of the areas of ministry where practice might appear to be cleanly split down lines of church tradition. However, the enormous pastoral value of a clearly identified rite in which a penitent expresses the specific reality of their need for forgiveness and receives words of absolution is now recognized well beyond the boundaries of its home tradition. Although many dioceses do not encourage or even allow the newly ordained to exercise this ministry, curates may valuably learn from the experience of their incumbents, in preparation for beginning to exercise the ministry themselves.

It is an area of ministry in which general ministerial skills and good practice are brought into particular focus. It's especially important to take at face value the words of the individual: if what lies on their conscience is important to them, don't belittle it. An over-formal environment may make them feel awkward, but on the other hand, to simply sit down for a chat without any formal words of liturgy or symbolic action or dress may disable their ability to recognize, and receive, the liberating ministry that Christ has committed to his Church.

Those from a Catholic tradition may be familiar with the rite, and may be encouraged to ensure that it is well offered, and not kept as a preserve for those who are widely regarded as premier Christians. Those from an evangelical or charismatic tradition, familiar with models of prayer ministry, should be aware that this particular form of ministry may be called for on occasion, and need not be avoided. It is helpful to set aside a time, and possibly a special place. Liturgy for the ministry of reconciliation is available from a number of sources, and it will probably be possible to incorporate prayer ministry and the laying on of hands within the rite.[4]

The Church has developed many different ministries, symbols, rites and liturgies throughout its history. They have arisen in response to need, and exist as pointers to the presence of God in the midst of pastoral relationships. In our present culture, we are fortunate that it is easier than ever before to draw from the whole spectrum of such traditions to bring whatever is appropriate for each person to find a way to open their lives to God.

What do you do when faith deserts you?

This chapter began with a call for integrity, but there are times when integrity would seem to lead us to stop halfway up the pulpit steps and return to our stalls, recognizing that faith just isn't there today; to come down from the altar to acknowledge the row we have had with the family on the way to church; to give up on ministry altogether in the light of a recurrent failing.

Candidates for ordination used to be encouraged with a doctrine of the Church's ministry that stated: 'even if you murdered your grandmother on Saturday night, on Sunday morning the mass is still the mass is still the mass. It doesn't depend on you!' This is not a view we would take today, but in fact it contains an important perspective. An ordained minister represents not just their own understanding and faith but the understanding and faith of the whole Church. This is not an excuse for lack of discipline, but it does recognize that the liturgy is there to hold us, and the congregation, true to our calling – and is much larger than our own daily perceptions.

Our own patterns of belief and ministry will develop over the years. This development will often happen through times of personal crisis, when we realize that what we have understood just does not fit our experience, or satisfy, any longer. At these times we may not 'feel like' exercising ministry: it is at these times that God in his Church holds us, while we continue to enable others to know of his hope and his love in the midst of our own questions.

6

Maturing into your vocation

The primary training relationship

John Witcombe

Of primary importance for all curates is the training relationship with their incumbent. It is the first of the concentric circles that constitute the context of the curacy. We looked at the significance of this relationship in Chapter 3 in the section on choosing a parish: here it is discussed from a different angle to explore its particular dynamic. Most curates will see more of their training incumbent than of any other member of the parish – more, probably, than of any member of their family or their friends.

Supervision

The training relationship is complex, and bears scrutiny. A curate will hope to receive inspiration, guidance, support and advice from their training incumbent, but they will also know that they should expect some degree of discipline. Reports are never far away, and no matter how much talk there is of collegiality, the incumbent ultimately holds the authority. However, power is not all on one side in this partnership: the incumbent is also looking for support, for a colleague, for fresh vision, and for some affirmation of their own skills and experience.

One of the best examinations of the complexities of this supervision relationship is found in David Lyall and John Foskett's *Helping the Helpers*. They show how the incumbent needs to balance a duty towards the trainee, the Church authorities, divine authority, and the parishioner: not an easy task, when the needs of one may apparently conflict with the needs of another. This is well illustrated in their work by the *clinical rhombus*, a model drawn from supervision in the health service:[1]

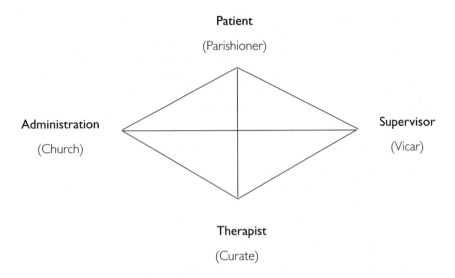

The authors also describe in detail how both incumbent and curate may respond to the task of exploring reported pastoral encounters. Past experience, for example, may have a powerful impact on both partners, but if this is unacknowledged it may be profoundly disabling, provoking reactions to a situation or conversation out of all proportion to the incident itself, but which if opened up can provide access to areas of past hurt which may be resolved or healed. Good supervision is at the heart of good training and development for both curate and incumbent: the process merits more preparation and reflection than is often found in the busyness of parish programmes. Many of those who are experienced in supervision would testify to the benefit of a consultant to maximize the opportunities that are present in a good working relationship, and to help avoid the dangers of communication breaking down.

Work consultants and working agreements

A facilitator who is contracted to sit with both parties on a regular basis to offer work consultancy will be a worthwhile appointment. Many dioceses have lists of those who have trained for such a role. It is worth investing in such an appointment at an early stage in the working relationship, even if it seems unnecessary at the time. As time moves on, most collegiate work will benefit from an external voice who can enable the parties to continue to listen well to one another, and to work towards implementing common vision. The facilitator should seek individual feedback from all team members before meeting with them, and offer assistance in working through issues that emerge.

A working agreement is another extremely valuable tool in facilitating the relationship between vicar and curate, and may usefully form the basis for the work of the facilitator. Some dioceses have 'standard format' working agreements that they promote. Areas covered typically include: mutual expectations; use of time; pattern of worship and prayer; personal and professional development; staff support; pastoral responsibility; administration and finance; conflict resolution; tenure of office; conditions of service; and review.

Working agreements are a valuable aid to communication, the most essential ingredient of a satisfactory working relationship. The effort of establishing such an agreement, either in preparation for the curacy or in its first few weeks, will pay dividends in later years.

Friends or colleagues?

It is a great joy when lasting friendship emerges out of a working relationship, but this is not inevitable. Hopes should run high in both parties as a curacy is approached, and opportunities may be created for such a friendship to blossom. Nevertheless, either party may be disappointed that their overtures of friendship do not seem to be met with a corresponding enthusiasm on the part of the other person. Incumbents may find that the current partnership fails to match up to its predecessor – in which case their curates may always feel that they have failed to find the place in the heart of their incumbent held by former colleagues. Curates may find themselves unable to meet their incumbent's expectations, and prefer to look to their contemporaries for support; or they may find that their supervisor prefers to keep a professional distance.

The relationship between the supervising incumbent and the curate needs to be that of an effective team, working with the wider ministry team in the parish. Much is now made of the value of collaborative ministry: this is the aim, and though friendship is to be welcomed, it is not the primary purpose of the relationship. There will always be times when curate and incumbent will see two different sides to a situation, and they need to be able to disagree – perhaps quite strongly – for the greater good of the parish. There will be times when each may wonder if they have been self-centred, or expressed poor judgement: they need the freedom for challenge in the relationship which a really close friendship might engender, but which a halfway house between colleague and friend may actually inhibit. It will, however, be important to invest strongly in the working partnership: in addition to the use of a work consultant, already mentioned, other ways of doing this are mentioned in Chapter 7.

Continuing ministerial education and your curacy

David Runcorn

Not so long ago the in-service programme that accompanied the first years of ordained ministry was formally called Post Ordination Training – and less reverently known as 'Potty Training'. The terminology betrayed the tendency to think of the task as being to tidy up any bits left over from the pre-ordination course and to ensure that basic ministerial functions were working well. Perhaps in a more settled age than ours some skills could be learned at the outset, once and for all. But in such a rapidly changing and unpredictable context as today's culture and Church it is essential to approach Christian ministry as a vocation to lifelong learning.

Continuing Ministerial Education (CME) is now the name given to the ministry training and development programmes in the Church of England. Its vision and task is 'to equip and develop the Church's ministers in order that they may stimulate and enable the whole Church to participate more fully in the mission of God in the world'.[2] CME 1–4 refers to the first phase of this learning process. It is 'continuing' because Christian formation has already been under way for some time prior to ordination and because our growing into the mystery and mercy of Christ's call is never finished. So although there will be aspects of CME 1–4 that are specific to the training needs of those beginning ordained ministry, it is the intention to establish a habit of continuous learning and resourcing that will sustain all Christians throughout their life and work.

The training context for CME

An introduction to the world of CME 1–4 needs prefacing with three general observations.

First, you are about to start life as an ordained minister in a Church that is committed to your nurture, development and training. This is an area that has received a considerable amount of professional planning and resourcing in recent years. National guidelines and agreed expectations are now in place.[3] These cover the establishing of basic competencies in areas such as pastoral relating, planning and leading public worship, leadership and pastoral skills, essential legal and organizational awareness, communication and preaching abilities, prayer and personal spiritual disciplines, and continuing theological study. In practice, dioceses vary in size, resources and numbers of curates, so the way they choose to structure their training programmes will vary too. It is likely that in the future CME 1–4 will be organized regionally.[4] This means that in the coming years we shall see more training resources shared across diocesan boundaries.

Second, you are beginning ordained ministry in a particular diocese that will have its own vision, priorities and strategy for ministry. This means in the first instance that you will find yourself working out your ministry development with a very mixed group of people. The variety is not so much one of church tradition as of different expressions of ministry. Routes to ordination are becoming increasingly varied, too. Some curates will have trained at residential colleges, some on regional courses. Some will already be highly experienced, while others feel very much beginners. Some will now be in full- or part-time stipendiary ministry in the Church while others will be continuing in their prior professional calling and may express their understanding of ministry in Church and society in very different ways. In the diocese in which I work, for example, stipendiary and non-stipendiary ministers and ordained local ministers train alongside each other, but other dioceses have developed different patterns of ministry. These factors will influence the shape and content of the training programme and the way it is delivered.

Third, you bring your own experience of life and work into the beginnings of ordained ministry. This is a generous and enriching gift that must not be underestimated. Your previous experience and training form the foundation on which continued learning and development is built. For some NSM and OLM curates who are continuing in their professional employment, this will be the continuing context in which ordained ministry is exercised and reflected upon.

For everyone, the task of integrating their previous experience into the life of ordained ministry is not simply a matter of transferring skills. A new relationship needs to be established, and this will take time. It can mean living, at times, with the uncomfortable feeling of being deskilled.[5] Whilst it is important that established skills and experience are honoured and valued, we need to be willing to become learners again if we are to begin to fulfil our vocation in this new ministry context.

The aims and content of training

So, once you are ordained, what can you expect from your CME 1–4 programme?

I have already mentioned how practical factors influence how the training is structured in any one diocese. One of the larger dioceses in the Church of England has 65 curates. It offers a rolling three-year programme structured around six weekend residential conferences. Each focuses on a specific area of ministry – spirituality, evangelism and mission, teamwork and leadership, pastoral care, faith and work, and communication and preaching. Every curate attends two weekends a year with their year group, shared with another year group. In addition there are several Ministerial Development Days each year. Some of these are on themes specific to a stage of ministry: for example, the deacon year may include some introductory training on pastoral boundaries or time management as well as giving time to reflect on the approaching ordination to priesthood. Early in the third year there will be opportunity to review the experience of ministry so far, to explore in which directions it might develop and to assess relevant training needs in the light of that. In common with other dioceses there are times when NSM, stipendiary and OLM curates have their own separate meetings to support each other in the distinctive expressions of ordained ministry.

Dioceses with fewer curates may not be able to provide such an extensive programme, but this is counterbalanced by more personal attention from diocesan staff and tutors, and a greater opportunity for curates to be able to set and negotiate the training agenda.

In most dioceses a system of peer support groups exists for all NSM and stipendiary curates[6] alongside the training programme. These typically meet every six weeks, in year groups, with a support group convenor who is an experienced parish priest.

Further training and study

Some curates are still working on a course of academic study which they will need time to complete in the first years of ministry. Others decide that the discipline of working towards an academic qualification is a helpful way of deepening theological reflection on ministry, or a particular aspect of it. A wide variety of such courses are available, though finding the funding for them is not getting any easier. Some dioceses discourage the pursuit of further academic qualifications outside the CME programme during the first year or two of a curacy. If you think you might wish to continue with academic study, it is wise to check the level of support that will be available from the diocese before ordination.

An academic course is not the only way to deepen your understanding of ministry. For some, a specialist placement or project with, for example, the local prison chaplaincy, school or youth centre may be a more effective means of achieving the same end.

All these possibilities should form part of your early discussions with your training incumbent and perhaps your CME director.

The goal of training

In close partnership with your training incumbent and the community in which you minister, the CME 1–4 programme aims to assist your ministry development in three particular ways.

1. By providing training and understanding for the core professional tasks of ordained ministry

The CME programme gives you the opportunity to consolidate, update or learn new skills in key areas of practical ministry. You will be introduced to the latest resources, and have the chance to listen to creative practitioners in different areas of ministry and to learn from other people's experiences.

It is also important to point out that your ministry is being lived out in a particular historic and theological expression of the Christian Church. As a minister you become a representative of this Church in a special way. This Church has its own organization, structures and ways of doing things. There are reasons for these. They will inevitably shape the way you 'do' ministry. They may need changing and renewing, but they need understanding first. You also begin ordained ministry at a particularly critical time in the life of this Church and of the culture in which it has long been embedded. How much does this mean to you? 'You are here because God wants you to be here. And God's wanting you to be here has been mediated to you through centuries of mixed and imaginative witness ... Be thankful for that witness, and how it has made the reality of God's welcome complete for you.'[7]

2. By strengthening your ability to work as a reflective practitioner

This is about the ability to think theologically, biblically and spiritually about the context of your ministry so as to discern the significance of what is going on in it. Someone once said, 'All theology, properly so called, is written in blood.' Theology is not the theory that we then apply to practical situations. Christian theology takes flesh. It is lived out in our humanity, in the joys and wounds of human experience.

In busy ministry the discipline of reflection is never easy to sustain but it is vital to struggle with it. It must be given time. Without it ministry can quickly become simply reactive – driven by the next immediate need or crisis. It will also help to protect us from a tendency to make 'short-term' responses to ministry. Under the pressures facing the Church today it is also very tempting to look for the latest solution or strategy 'off the shelf' that promises to deliver what we seek. Writing within a tradition renowned for its frenetic activism, Eugene Petersen was urging the need for the same qualities when he called for the development of 'the Contemplative Pastor'.[8] Reflective practice is the soil in which the core spiritual gift of discernment can grow. There is no substitute for it in ministry.

3. By deepening and enriching the disciplines that nurture your own personal and spiritual development

Christian ministry today requires a high degree of personal, psychological, spiritual and relational awareness and integration. What this means in practice will vary from person to person, but to assist in its development is a priority of any training programme. This is another area that has been given serious thought and resourcing in recent years, and rightly so.[9]

One reason for the demands that ordained ministry places upon us is the complexity of who we are called to be in the community. The ordained minister is a representative spiritual figure, even in an increasingly marginalized Church. Considerable expectations and hopes are placed on us, though they are not usually acknowledged. We are asked to fulfil a variety of possibly contradictory roles in the community. At a conference of clergy who had all recently become incumbents, a number of them spoke of times when they felt as if they had lost their personal identity: 'Who am I in all this?' The role and the demands of being this representative person had felt quite overwhelming. (See the fuller discussion of this subject in the next chapter.)

Pastoral ministry also requires us to develop our relational skills. It has been said that 'the last thing we realize about ourselves is our effect'. I remember feeling terribly hurt when, as a new vicar, I presented my vision and plans to my church council. Instead of being impressed and grateful, several of them were openly angry with me. The meeting got nowhere and I left feeling hurt and bruised. It is not enough to have good intentions: we all need people who can help us understand how we come across. We are not usually very good at recognizing the effect we have on others, so we may need to seek out people who will speak truth to us in love.

Our prayer and spiritual lives may need to develop in new ways. We will need help to think creatively about our spiritual resourcing. It is no failure to find that patterns of faith and prayer that sustained us in the past no longer work for us. We will need to go exploring. This requires time and planning for: we don't grow spiritually by chance. Most of us recognize when we are physically exhausted or emotionally weary. It is harder to discern when our spiritual energies are running low, and the work of ministry can leave us running on empty for some time before we realize what has happened.

What do *you* want?

Despite all that has been said above about what a good CME 1–4 programme can provide as you grow into ministry, there may be more important questions to ask: What do *you* want? What are *you* looking for? What is *your* vision for the development of your ministry, and where do you discern your own needs for ongoing training?

These are exciting and demanding times to be in Christian ministry. The challenge is to think boldly and imaginatively and to take risks. The first three or four years of ordained ministry provide an opportunity to do this – it will not be so possible once you take on more specific leadership responsibilities. CME will hopefully be one of the things that provokes, widens and excites your vision of what ministry can be by God's grace.

For these few short years the buck does not stop with you. There is a chance to explore and to venture outside the familiar securities of established skills and experience. I have long loved the reply of an 85-year-old woman when asked what she might do differently if she could live her life over again: 'I would try to make more mistakes next time. I would take more chances.' As you contemplate the early years of your ministry, what mistakes would it be good to make?

When Henri Nouwen wanted to express the heart of Christian discipleship he turned to his lifelong love of circus trapeze artists. They became for him an image of the adventure of faithful living. 'I can only fly freely', he wrote, 'when I know there is a catcher to catch me. If we are to take risks, in the air, in life, we have to know there's a catcher.' This requires a radical letting go. And you must allow yourself to be caught – the catching and securing is not something you can do for yourself. If you try to save your own life you will lose it. Trust the catcher.

Professional and spiritual support

Claire Pedrick and Diane Clutterbuck

Ordinands are now expected to find and use a spiritual director or soul friend during their initial ministerial education. This helps to set the pattern for the whole of their ministry. A good spiritual director can challenge you to push at the boundaries of your faith in and experience of God, and to make sense of the different stages you go through. You may find that you need to change spiritual director from time to time as your perception of yourself and your ministry changes.

Some dioceses have a register of spiritual directors, and an experienced director who will discuss with you the sort of person you are looking for. They will then suggest someone who they think will fit your needs, and arrange a meeting for you with that person, so that the two of you can explore the possibility of working together. In other dioceses the CME adviser will know how to contact spiritual directors in your area. If your diocese does not have a process for spiritual direction you will have to arrange your own. The National Retreat Associatio[10] can put you in touch with someone in your area who knows people who act as spiritual directors.

What would you look for in a spiritual director?

There is within the churches (it is good to look beyond your own denomination) a deep reservoir of listening people, both lay and ordained, who are experienced spiritual directors. They vary enormously in their background and approach, so you need to think carefully about what you are looking for in a spiritual director, as different things matter to different people. You might like to consider the following questions:

- Would you prefer a man or a woman, and should they be older, younger, or about the same age as you?

- Would you prefer them to be ordained or lay, Anglican or from another denomination, from a particular tradition, such as Anglo-Catholic, evangelical, Franciscan, Benedictine, Ignatian or charismatic?

- Is it important that your spiritual director shares your interest in poetry, hymnody, the Desert Fathers, gardening, art or music?

A spiritual director who is very different from you will bring challenge and insight; working with someone from your own tradition might provide a supportive mentor. Over time, clergy often look for a new spiritual director who will bring a new perspective. What's right for you now? Is this the person who will help you develop over the next few years? Might this person be someone you already know, or a stranger you will not meet in other contexts?

What happens next?

Finding the right person to act as your spiritual director is a delicate business and can take time. Once you have found someone you feel happy with and who is happy to work with you, it's helpful either at or before your first meeting to negotiate a clear contract which sets out details of the frequency of your meetings, their location (how far are you prepared to travel to meet your director? – some people drive quite a distance, in order to have thinking time in the car), and the fee if one is to be paid. For some people the spiritual director also acts as a coach or work consultant because that is what has been agreed; for others, the scope of the conversation can be more general. Negotiating the nature of your relationship will help you both to be clear about its purpose, and about what you hope to achieve through it.

At your first encounter, in addition to these specifics you are likely to talk about your spiritual journey so far and how you'll manage your relationship. Spiritual direction is not an interrogation. The focus will be on your agenda, and your spiritual director will not be telling you what to do but will give you a framework of accountability before God. Spiritual direction is not therapy, it is a three-way encounter: you, the director, and God. It is not usual for spiritual directors to hear the confessions of their directees, but they may do this if it is appropriate.

The focus of spiritual direction is on the whole of life lived in the context of a relationship with God. God is at the centre. A good spiritual director will help you to work at your relationship with God by encouraging questioning and reflection so that you are able to discern more clearly the way God is at work in your life and where he is leading you.

Other sources of help

In addition to spiritual direction, several dioceses also offer work consultants or ministry consultants who work with clergy to reflect on certain aspects of their ministry. These people are usually experienced practitioners who are not there to give advice or tell clergy what to do but are there to listen, ask questions and provide space where clergy can find their own answers to issues that concern them. The person responsible for CME in your diocese will be able to tell you what is on offer. If there is no formal diocesan scheme there are independent coaches who work with clergy on a range of issues arising from their work and vocation.

Some spiritual directors are part of a religious community. This may well allow you to see them in the context of a quiet day or short retreat, and will encourage you to know that you are being prayed for by a community. You are also less likely to run in and out between other pressing engagements in these circumstances. Spiritual direction can be an integral part of quiet days or retreats, but these are also immensely valuable on their own as part of ongoing professional development.

Most parishes allow time for retreats and quiet days as part of the clergy year. Attitudes to such days vary according to different personalities. Whereas the person with a preference to be an organized introvert (I and J in terms of Myers-Briggs) might have reflection time written into their diary for the whole year, people with a preference for extroversion may develop mixed feelings about time spent alone and how they will benefit from quiet. The purpose of retreats is time away, time to reflect and time to be with God. One church worker found this by booking into a B&B and walking round the town for a couple of days in reflective mode. Clergy in your local chapter will have ideas of where to go for retreats, and the National Retreat Association can also provide information about venues and events.

Immense support can also be gained from colleagues, both locally and nationwide. Meeting clergy from a broader area can offer support, challenge, the opportunity to gain ideas, and new networks. Locally this can be found in the deanery and the diocese. It is worth investing time in meeting other clergy, since this gives a larger picture of the Church in a particular area across all Anglican traditions. Clergy chapters provide an ecumenical link in your parish or town. Some clergy sit on diocesan synods and choose to take the larger picture by standing for General Synod. For priests whose ministerial development will take them beyond parish ministry, it is crucial to have an understanding of regional and national issues as well as networking more widely. Most jobs are advertised, but if you have an interest, for example, in theological education, it is critical to know people in that area who can advise you and, if appropriate, champion your cause.

Conferences and day training events are very important: commit yourself to a pattern of attending these, e.g. CME, New Wine Network or Affirming Catholicism. It is tremendously important to gain fresh ideas, and the support and networking opportunities these occasions provide are not to be underestimated. Reading groups, for clergy or 'mixed' groups, are a good way of studying with others.

Looking ahead

CME and ministerial development raise questions about how to prepare for future posts. It would be naïve to think that every curate reading this book will stay in parish ministry until retirement: that may be your dream, or you may be nurturing other ambitions. A senior cleric was horrified recently to meet a curate who expressed the desire to become a bishop. Why? In the business world, graduate trainees who are keen to develop their careers are seen as an asset, and ambition for promotion is perceived as a strength. In the Church, the curate who articulated a similar desire was received with confusion and surprise – yet someone wishing to move to a bigger church after their curacy is seen as acceptable. What's the difference?

Self-centred ambition is counter to any concept of vocation, yet some degree of ambition is as essential an ingredient of ministry as is some stress. Without any ambition, we can easily suffer from a lack of energy, drive and direction. But is there such a thing as holy ambition?

Holy ambition helps us to set our sights higher than we might normally set them. It inspires vision, excellence, energy, motivation, and it can lead to the development of the Church, its projects and its people. It is not about getting to the top for me, to enhance my status, to build my empire, but about being motivated to greater and deeper acts of service.

Unholy ambition isn't new: Esau and Jacob jostled for position, Joseph had dreams of greatness, and even the disciples argued about who would be the greatest in the kingdom of God. Unholy or self-centred ambition has its ugly side: the desire to win at all costs – mine must be the best church and I must get the best job; the tendency to become dissatisfied with the present – and always be looking ahead to the next job; the need to engage in self-promotion, to use others as a stepping stone, and always to be looking for the next step up. Holy ambition, on the other hand, puts other people first, and is always looking for ways of furthering the rule and work of God in the Church and in individual lives. The fruits of holy ambition are 'love, joy, peace, patience, kindness, goodness, faithfulness, gentleness and self-control' (Galatians 5.22).

Maintaining a balance between holy ambition and selfish ambition is a challenge, and one which reinforces the need for a supportive spiritual life. Taking time out through quiet days or retreats to look at the bigger picture – of ministry and of vocation – is key to maintaining this balance, as is accountability to friends or to a spiritual director who will tell the truth and not massage the ego.

Our motives will always be mixed: we have a vocation, and we're human beings. We can view our future ministry in at least two ways: as goal-centred – I want to be a bishop — or as possibility-centred — I could be a bishop. Ambition must include both vocation and servant leadership.

There are many ways in which the calling to the priesthood can be explored and skills and gifts developed through particular roles, encounters and through CME. While the majority of clergy will spend their whole ministry in parish-based roles, as well as senior posts there are also opportunities in diocesan jobs, sector ministry, overseas mission, chaplaincy, theological education, research, and secular employment. Roles like these will use skills you may have acquired in your previous career, and will develop new skills within you. One of the questions that have often been raised by those in sector ministry outside the parish is: What is sacramental about the work that I am doing? If you are a priest with a dual vocation — to ministry and accountancy, to hospital chaplaincy and management, to training or entrepreneurial business — you will need to explore what is distinctive about being a priest in this role. It's a challenging question which may require support from a spiritual director or a work consultant. Perhaps this is another area where being part of a network of other clergy in such roles is invaluable. If there is no difference between you and everyone else in the workplace, is this the right place to be?

Vocation is a dynamic journey. Whatever form of work or ministry you move through in your life as a priest, Meister Eckhart's words will ring true:

> The outward work can never be small if the inward one is great, and the outward work can never be great or good if the inward is small or of little worth.

For further reading

Everybody will be looking for different resources, depending on where their own particular journey is leading them. The suggestions which follow are, therefore, both few in number and necessarily 'generic' in nature.

Mark Barrett, *Crossing: Reclaiming the Landscape of our Lives*, Darton, Longman & Todd, 1991.

Monica Brown, *Embodying the God we Proclaim*, Kevin Mayhew, 2000.

Olivier Clement, *The Roots of Christian Mysticism*, New City, 1998.

Bruce Duncan, *Pray Your Way*, Darton, Longman & Todd, 1993.

Gerard W. Hughes, *God of Surprises*, Darton, Longman & Todd, 1992.

Basil Hume OSB, *Searching for God*, Hodder & Stoughton, 1977.

William Johnston, *Being in Love*, Fount, 1988.

Christopher Moody, *Eccentric Ministry*, Darton, Longman & Todd, 1992.

Henri Nouwen, *In the Name of Jesus,* Darton, Longman & Todd, 1989.

W. H. Vanstone, *Love's Endeavour, Love's Expense*, Darton, Longman & Todd, 1977.

Rowan Williams, *Silence and Honey Cakes: the wisdom of the desert*, Lion, 2003.

7

Self-management

Claire Pedrick and Diane Clutterbuck

Christians in the workplace are challenged by the sacred–secular divide, where what happens at work can seem disconnected from what happens at home. That isn't God's way, but it's easy for us to split our time into work and leisure, where the latter may be spent around the church and church community. Although technology has blurred the edges and made virtual working possible, geography often reinforces the boundaries between the workplace and leisure and home time: either you're at work, or you're at home. In ministry, those boundaries can become blurred. Your work and your worship come together in a different way. This can be positive and creative; it can also be challenging and even dangerous.

The *Guidelines for the Professional Conduct of the Clergy* draw attention to this directly:

> The bishop and those exercising pastoral care of the clergy should both by word and example actively encourage the clergy to adopt a healthy lifestyle. This should include adequate time for leisure, through taking days off and their full holiday entitlement, developing interests outside their main areas of ministry, and maintaining a commitment to the care of themselves and their personal relationships. Helping the clergy understand and overcome unrealistic expectations within themselves and from the outside world needs to be a priority.[1]

One of the most vivid and distressing illustrations of work/life imbalance you could imagine was presented on a course for priests who had been ordained for ten years. Jack drew a diagram on the flip chart of a cake that was divided into eight pieces, and he labelled each piece with an aspect of his ministry: pastoral work, preparation for worship, preparation and attending meetings, administration, and so on until all aspects of his work had been covered. He then drew a ninth segment and tried to fit this into the 'cake'. It wouldn't go, no matter how hard he tried. That segment was labelled 'family'.

Health check

It's time to take stock. On a scale of 10 – 0 (10 being very satisfied, 0 being not at all satisfied), how do you feel about these different aspects of your life?

- Working from home

- Work

- Partner and family (or your support network if you are single)

- Spiritual development

- Leisure

- Friends and community

- Money

- Health

Which are the areas where you need to focus your attention? And what personal and professional support do you need to enable you to function well? Self-management is about paying enough attention to all parts of your life so that you are able to fulfil your ministry effectively.

Know yourself

It would be wonderful if someone discovered a formula for self-management that suited everyone equally well – a 'one-size-fits-all' system. However, in spite of the large number of books currently available on time management, no one has yet (or ever will) come up with a formula that suits everyone, so you need to invest a bit of time in finding out what works for you. It is important for clergy to gather as much information as possible about their preferences for working and leisure patterns, not just in relation to the curate's role and getting the work done, but in order to engender personal growth and development.

There are a great many products on the market to enable individuals and teams to discover for example, more about their personality types, how they prefer to learn and how they work in a team. Most people in ministry will have encountered some of these during their theological training.

Myers Briggs Type Indicator®

Isabel Myers and Kathryn Briggs based the MBTI® on the observations of the psychiatrist Carl Jung and the results of more than 20 years of their own research. They devised a framework to help people understand why they behave the way they do. The MBTI® questionnaire is based on a personality framework that helps people to explore their preferences for:

- taking in information

- making decisions

- focusing their attention

- how they live their lives – their preferred way of working and interacting with people.

MBTI®[2] helps people to understand themselves better. Once you know your type preference it can tell you about your attitude to a variety of things, including:

- personal development: learning style and motivation, career development, leadership style, team role, time and stress management, coaching;

- team building and team development: improving communication, enhancing problem solving, valuing diversity and resolving conflict;

- organizational change: understanding and working with response to change, understanding team and corporate culture.

Learning styles

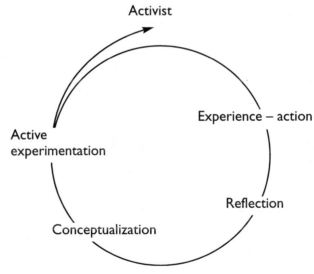

Fig. I   Kolb's Learning Cycle

Kolb's learning cycle (see Figure I) demonstrates four different aspects of learning: Experience; Reflection; Conceptualization; and Active Experimentation. Each of these stages in the learning cycle relates to styles or preferences for learning. This is most obvious in 'Reflection', the second element of the learning cycle, which has the same name as its learning style. A person whose preferred style of learning is reflection will feel most comfortable with that part of the learning cycle; they may not feel quite so comfortable moving on to the next stage, of drawing conclusions through conceptualization!

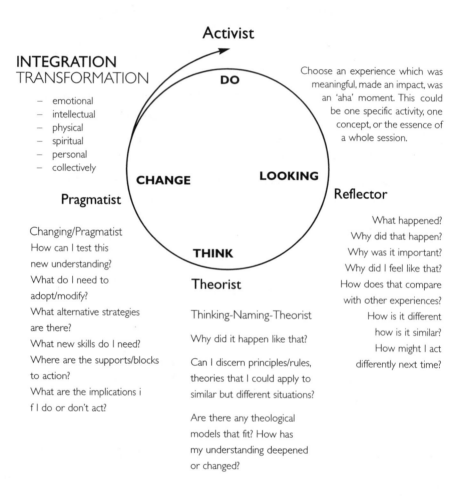

Activist

INTEGRATION
TRANSFORMATION

- emotional
- intellectual
- physical
- spiritual
- personal
- collectively

DO

Choose an experience which was meaningful, made an impact, was an 'aha' moment. This could be one specific activity, one concept, or the essence of a whole session.

CHANGE   **LOOKING**

Pragmatist   ### Reflector

Changing/Pragmatist
How can I test this new understanding?
What do I need to adopt/modify?
What alternative strategies are there?
What new skills do I need?
Where are the supports/blocks to action?
What are the implications i f I do or don't act?

THINK

Theorist

Thinking-Naming-Theorist

Why did it happen like that?

Can I discern principles/rules, theories that I could apply to similar but different situations?

Are there any theological models that fit? How has my understanding deepened or changed?

What happened?
Why did that happen?
Why was it important?
Why did I feel like that?
How does that compare with other experiences?
How is it different how is it similar?
How might I act differently next time?

(The life-long spirals of learning: action/reflection learning model based on Kolb and Solberg and experiences in the CCS Core Learning Groups)

Fig.2 The Action/Reflection Learning Cycle

The same can also be said of the other elements of the cycle. The person whose preference is for activism will find experience playing an important part in their learning. The theorist will be most at home with the part of the cycle in which conceptualization takes place. The pragmatist learner will be keen to get on to the application of what is learned.

This does not mean that people can only participate in one element of the learning cycle. All learning must involve all elements, but because people may have a tendency to feel satisfied by one aspect of the cycle more than others, this may actually limit their learning, because they may be inclined to stop at that point rather than complete the cycle.

The learning cycle points to the value of learning in a group. In a church context this is one practical way in which Paul's image of the church as a body in 1 Corinthians 12, with its mutually dependent members, works out in practice. In groups where there is a mixture of people who represent the four preferred learning styles, and where each of the styles is valued, people will have very rich learning experiences which will always lead to growth and some kind of action. In teams it is important for each member to know and understand the preferred learning styles of other team members. If a team is made up of people who are activists and theorists, they will find reflection particularly difficult and may often miss it out altogether.

The value of this understanding is to enable any communicator to remember the cycle in their own individual learning, in the development and work done by a clergy or ministry team, in parish groups and with other curates in CME 1–4. It's not uncommon to find groups stuck in the conceptualization mode. Our experience is that seeing the cycle and pointing out where a group is stuck whilst at the same time encouraging them to look at the next process can unblock groups effectively and allow them to move forward.

Working from home

> Will you strive to fashion your own life and that of your household according to the way of Christ?[3]

The house

Apart from NSMs and OLMs, who are likely to remain in their own homes, curates are likely to move into new accommodation, which may have been used by previous post-holders before. If that is the case, the house will be familiar to church members and they are likely to feel at home there. How do you establish this house as *your* home and workplace?

For many curates, this will be the first time they have ever worked from home, so this is the time to set up working patterns that will serve you for the rest of your ministry. This is the chance to get it right. How will you work from home? Will you impose your choice on the way things are done, or will you just let things emerge and see how it goes? Whatever your preferred mode of working, regular review of how things are going is an important part of developing an individual style that works.

Public or private?

When parishioners visit, they will know where the kitchen is, and the toilet. They'll also know how the previous curate used the building. You are not the previous curate!

You will need to make some decisions, with your family if you have one, about the extent to which your house is going to be used as a public place. Not everyone will be comfortable with the traditional model of the 'open all hours' vicarage. Look at the layout of the rooms. If the best room for a study is upstairs, where will you see people for one-to-one conversations? Anything is possible as you move into a house. For those for whom open house is an important part of their ministry, a bedroom could become a sitting room to allow other family members to withdraw from the hubbub of visitors. Single curates might use an upstairs room for retreat if they have made the downstairs of the house a very public area.

Jackie started a curacy after many years of academic life as a student and lecturer. A one-bedroomed flat seemed like luxury after a university room, but combining study, leisure and parish in one room became claustrophobic quite quickly.

It's important to guard your privacy, and that of your family if you have one. It may be possible to eat in the kitchen. A dining room might be used for entertaining, but could provide a second living area where the parish don't go. A clearly defined work space can stop parish life haemorrhaging into home life. Starting to think outside the box usually provides several different ways of configuring the rooms in a house to make the space work for you and everyone else who lives there.

In the excitement of a new start, remember that you and your family have your own legitimate needs. The parish might have its own ideas of what the house should be used for – as an extra parish room, perhaps – but how far is this really necessary? There might be nowhere to use in the church building, but pubs have upstairs rooms and parishioners have homes that could be used to meet such needs.

When Pete and his wife moved into their curate's house, they decided to make the downstairs public and the upstairs private. They have a sitting room downstairs where they host meetings and welcome guests, and another sitting room upstairs which is their own space. Some evenings, the parish meet downstairs while Pete and Joy are watching a DVD upstairs!

Working space

Do you keep your working space contained, or does it spread far and wide around the house? How you use your working space, or space in the house for working, will affect you and those who live with you. If you are one of those who leave sermon preparation in the living room and parish files on the side in the kitchen, they will still be in view during your leisure time, which will make it much harder to switch off. This will affect you and may drive the others who live in the house with you insane. Even if you choose to work in different parts of the house, it can be helpful to return books and papers to the office when you finish work in order to make a clear boundary between working and non-working time. This can be the only way to keep work in its place. You could make some simple rules for yourself that everyone else will understand: if I'm in the office, I'm working; if I'm not (and the door is closed), I'm not working.

One of the most difficult tensions in ministry is that the curate may feel they are available to the family if they are at home when in fact they are not. Or others might think they are busy when in fact they are playing Spider Solitaire or tweaking PowerPoint. John Bell of the Iona Community once said that many ministers have a mistress – it's the computer! They spend hours on rotas, worship sheets, magazines, etc. that they should be spending with their families. We kid ourselves that it's important. Is it always?

Even if work isn't physically intruding, it's often only on holidays or days out that clergy switch off and are really there for their family.

Meetings

You are going to have meetings. Some will be with individuals, others with groups. They might need to be held in your house, or there might be an office or suitable room away from the house that you can use. Be especially careful if the meeting is with someone of the opposite sex. Sometimes, the best place to meet is somewhere neutral, like a hotel lobby, where a quiet, confidential conversation can happen in a public place.

If you choose to meet in your home, it's important to ask if it is for your convenience or the convenience of others. How do the people who share the house with you feel about you having meetings at home? Even after a meeting has finished, it may take a long time – even days – for the space to feel as if it belongs to the family again. This is partly about association of space and task: what do you think of as you walk into a room – does your intuition say 'this is a place to relax', or 'this is a place to work', or even 'this is a place where I had a challenging work conversation'? These subconscious feelings will be informed and fed by our experience of how that space has been used in the past.

Study or office?

What do you need from your working space?

- A place to think and pray

- A place to write

- A place to read

- A place to meet individuals

- A place to hold meetings

- A place of calm to escape to

- A place to store books and information

- Any combination of the above

The question 'How do I arrange my office/study?' is one of the most important a curate will ask. The answer may change as ministry changes, and it is worth asking yourself the question again from time to time. You might, in fact, not do your best thinking in the house at all! Some people find more inspiration in a coffee shop or on a walk – in which case a notebook or a dictaphone can be useful. Or you can ring yourself up and leave a message on your own answerphone if a good idea occurs to you on a walk or car journey.

How many functions will your office/study have to fulfil? It's hard to be reflective on an office chair in front of a computer screen, so if you want to use the space as a study as well, what do you need in there for it to be a place where you will be able to relax and pray? If you want to use the room primarily as an office, where will you do your praying and your reading?

Some clergy use this room to pray. If this is not the right room, is there somewhere in your house that you could turn into a small private chapel, or a prayer corner, where you can pray, read the Bible and find space for reflection and listening to God? This might not need to happen in your study. Whatever space you have, think about what furniture, pictures and other things you will need to make this your place to pray.

If the room is big enough, there may be space for an armchair and a couple of desks – one for creative thought and one for administration. Realistically, though, this might need to wait for your post of first responsibility and a purpose-built vicarage!

Only when a decision has been made about whether this room is study or office or a combination of both will it be clear what furniture will be needed in there.

Hilary was the CME Adviser for a small diocese. A large part of her work was done with a group of about 20 curates. Hilary found that she spent a great deal of time talking with them on the telephone. Knowing that she concentrates best when she is comfortable and relaxed – something she rarely achieves at her desk – in the corner of her home office she created an area around the telephone furnished with big floor cushions, a low table, a lamp and a supply of paper and pencils. Here she could comfortably talk with the curates for as long as was needed, free from distractions.

Equipment

The equipment in your working space doesn't need to be fancy, but it does need to work for you. A worktop area, drawers and storage space are likely to be the minimum requirements. This might be a family heirloom desk, or a cheap set-up made from MDF and battens or bricks. If finances are difficult at the start of your curacy, a good way of developing suitable equipment is to use cardboard boxes for storage until you find a system that works for you. Think about what needs to be on your desk and what needs to be near at hand. How much book shelving do you need? It may be that you choose to keep all your books in the study/office, or there may be space for some elsewhere.

A filing cabinet is a great tool for people who will put things into it. If you are always going to be a person who has piles on the floor, what do you need to make your papers safe and accessible? It may simply be another cardboard box!

A computer is increasingly essential – but only if it works for you. The same thing applies to an electronic organizer. Many people convert to electronic and find the address book is great, but they can't see their diary. If that's you, perhaps the organizer was a good investment as an up-to-date contacts list – and you can go back to a paper diary with a clear conscience.

It saves money if you try out ideas before you buy new furniture. It's easy to poach an armchair from another room for a couple of weeks to establish whether you really will read in it if you put one there, or if it will just become another storage surface!

Telephone: friend or foe?

The telephone is an important tool and a significant enemy to anyone in parish ministry. It is invasive, so managing the telephone from day one is crucial for both clergy and parish. However much the ring of the telephone might be exciting in the first few weeks, it's very important to ensure that it remains a tool that works for you and never becomes your enemy.

Only give out your mobile number to the people you really want to have it. Some curates are given mobiles by the parish but retain a personal mobile for private use. Then the parish telephone can be left at home on days off and holidays and a very good boundary is set up. Many priests have found enormous value in installing a second land line or having a dedicated number for personal use only. Never give this to anyone who might pass it on to church members! And if calls ever do come in on parish business, ask them to call the other number. That sets effective boundaries. Be careful of making outbound calls on your personal line, or 1471 might give your number away.

An answerphone is essential and must be used to support the boundaries that you have established, especially at meal times and other family times. It might be possible to divert calls to the parish office occasionally, if there is one. If you are in a pastoral situation with a parishioner, the mobile must be switched off. Family and friends deserve the same!

Managing time and tasks

It's not unusual for anyone with a responsible job to have half a mind on it when they're at home. What is distinctive for clergy and others who work from home, which will include many in your parish, is that at home you are still physically in the workplace. Therefore as well as thinking about issues, sermons or a myriad of other priorities, it's also possible to get re-involved during non-working time. The only difference between you and your parishioners who work from home is that your home may be more defined as a public space.

Creating effective boundaries is a challenge for all. Others working from home make it possible by imposing careful boundaries on space and time. As a priest it's important to recognize the pressures upon you that are shared with other professionals within the parish, otherwise the division between you and the congregation, those in so-called 'secular' jobs, will grow. It seems to be the case that those who recognize the commonality of parts of priestly ministry with other professions are able to learn and share ideas with others and thereby reduce some of the pressure that can come from within them.

For the new curate who has spent time in the academic world of college or course training, the temptation to throw every ounce of their time and energy into the practical work of the parish is a strong one. A training post is a way of setting patterns for the future, however, so a degree of caution is an advisable accompaniment to enthusiasm.

Managing time can thus be one of the greatest challenges that clergy face. Some people find it easy – they are often the ones who write the time management books. For most of us, it's more difficult. In ministry, there is never enough time to do all the work that needs to be done. There will always be more you could do – it goes with the territory. Most 'off the shelf' time management schemes won't suit your precise needs, so try out different techniques and find out what does work. Many people have found rotating tasks to be a very effective way of managing multiplicity. Rather than working on one task exhaustively and for long periods of time, you allocate a limited amount of time to several tasks and rotate them so that you are focusing on each task for 20–30 minutes, before moving on to the next. You might divide up a hour into four segments and make headway with four tasks thus reducing the sense that important jobs are hanging over you.[4] Some people value a rhythm of work – starting with prayer, desk and study in the morning, visiting in the afternoon, meetings in the evening. Others work differently again. For clergy with children or a partner who goes out to work, the timetables of family members can provide a helpful framework around which to build the day. If you are single, you need to consider building a framework for yourself, which may include time with friends, a walk, or a trip to the gym.

There is so much to do – it's vital to reiterate that. Some people love to do lists, others write them and never look at them again. Think of ways of managing priorities which have worked in the past and use them again. Managing a diary is a good step:

- Find a diary that works for you. It may be electronic or paper but it's important to be able to see more than a day at a time so that you can plan effectively. Seven days to view is best.

- Plan your time off and put it into your new diary as soon as you get it.

- Only write in your diary in pencil (or consume lots of Tippex).

- Be aware of people who say: 'Just put this in your diary.' That can turn into necessity. First ask: Do I need/want to be there? Am I able to be there? Let your yes be yes and your no be no!

- Don't take your diary to church — so you can't be bounced into putting things into it.

Procrastination may be the thief of time — it's also the gremlin of many people who work from an office or study at home. Learn to distinguish what are your real priorities.

- What is urgent and important?

- What is important but not urgent?

- What is urgent but not important?

- And what is neither urgent nor important?

Most of the time the urgent things will take up our time until you find you are simply managing one crisis after another. You need to find ways of spending time on and making space for the important but not urgent, as herein lie the activities and tasks that will feed you and help you to grow and develop.

A curacy is a time to experiment, under the supervision of your training incumbent, in order to find out how you work best and what works for you. If you need help, ask for it. There may be CME courses available that will help you. Some dioceses provide an assisted self-assessment scheme where clergy can reflect, with volunteers, on their ministry in a confidential setting.

Your relationship with your training incumbent

Curates tend to swing between either loving or hating their training incumbents, but a successful and healthy relationship is usually found somewhere between the two. Some incumbents will follow a good model of supervision and mentoring that works for you; others may be new to the role; others may have developed a style that doesn't suit you. In all cases, the relationship will be strengthened by good communication — you need to show your training incumbent how to manage you.

Finding the correct balance of how much time curates and incumbents need to spend together will develop as the relationship grows. It is valuable to go away for planning days and to participate in conferences together. As in any close working relationship, having meals together can be productive, as can meeting socially over a meal with spouses and children.

Depending on churchmanship, curates and training incumbents may pray together using daily offices or in a more informal way. Where that takes place and how it happens will need to be negotiated.

In any close working relationship, particularly in mixed gender teams, care needs to be taken that clear boundaries are established and observed. Not all affairs are sexual, and close working relationships can sometimes overstep those boundaries. In any situation with a training incumbent, if you have a sense of unease, do something about it. That may involve moving meetings into a more public place, or if necessary talking to the person responsible for CME.

How does your work affect your close relationships?

Whatever your family circumstances, your close relationships play a significant part in who you are. We looked at some of these in Chapter 4, in relation to the 'being' of being a curate; here we revisit the subject from a somewhat different angle.

Single clergy

If you live alone, paying attention to all aspects of your life is crucial. Slipping into habits of never having proper time off is easy when there is no one at home to remind you to stop working. And beware the expectations of parishioners who may assume you're available 24/7 because you are single.

During training you are likely to have found support networks amongst fellow students and also among those in the church or work community. In a first curacy, you will find yourself in a different situation, and suddenly church and work and friends are all rolled into one.

For those who wish to see old friends on days off, it's good to consider which day to take. It may be good to run several days off together if travel is involved. Finding support structures locally might include joining a sports club, a reading group, even a singles group. Or there may be other curates within easy reach with whom it's possible to develop a life outside the parish. Sustaining existing friendships from a distance will take time. If this is important to you, you will need to make it a priority. However useful email and texting are, remember to include some human contact with friends – something that is more than virtual.

Ordination and ministry have brought you into the public sphere. Whether you like it or not, you will be observed in this new role by both parishioners and neighbours. If you are in a relationship, you will need to think carefully about how you conduct that relationship. If you are in the early stages of a relationship, you may find it necessary to conduct that relationship outside the parish and to guard your privacy for as long as you possibly can. It helps to have confidants in the parish leadership who are supportive of your personal life. These people will also be publicly supportive if necessary, helping others to recognize your need to have a personal life and the space and 'time out' that that necessarily involves.

If you continue to develop a close relationship, you will need to reassure those who are aware of this that things shared with you, as a minister, in confidence will stay with you, and not be shared with your new partner. The same confidentiality issues emerge as would with a spouse (see the section on confidentiality, below). You will need to make it clear in your conversations with others (just as you would with a spouse) that to say something to one of you is not a short cut to saying it to both.

Married clergy

More than one vocation

Husbands and wives have their own vocations. (There can be a vocation to be a priest's wife or husband, but that is not an expectation.) A partner might be fully supportive of a curate's work, or they might prefer to stand on the sidelines. The curate's spouse is not the curate. This may sound obvious, but you may need to return to that idea during your ministry. Arriving in a new parish, you might find other people's expectations challenging or disconcerting. The role of partners in any marriage is to allow free development of each other's vocations, whatever they might be. It is very dangerous to see one vocation as more divinely appointed than another.

In some couples both partners have a vocation to the ordained ministry, and you may be married to an incumbent, another curate or someone in theological training. As we saw in Chapter 3, couples with a vocation to ordination can express a desire or calling to minister together, and it is not unreasonable to hope for a stipend each. However, that calling from God has to be balanced with the realities of ministry. Each partner needs to be good at the jobs for which they apply, and jobs need to come up at roughly the same time if there will be a significant geographical move. Although the ideal place for a couple to work might seem to be in a team ministry, the dynamics of a team with a married couple can raise fears and assumptions which, however unreasonable, might be a challenge that teams are reluctant to take on.

The reality for couples with a dual vocation to ministry is that the Church of England will do what it can, but it has no obligation to place you together. This is also true in the secular workplace. Some clergy couples work in situations where one partner has a parochial appointment and the other a sector ministry post (or both hold dual-role appointments). The Ministry Division has produced some guidelines on the deployment of clergy couples.

Jan and Bob were both ordained priests and expressed a desire to serve together in a parish. Having come from well-salaried jobs with many gifts, skills and talents, and with three teenage children to support, it was important to them for their own sense of self that they both found stipendiary posts. Both had come into ministry hoping to do parish work, but after several months of exploration, Jan took a parish job and Bob found a job as a hospital chaplain. It was the only way they could find what they wanted.

It is hard to balance multiple demands on your time and energy. And it is important to invest in your relationship. Many clergy have found that a good maxim is to treat your partner better than you treat your parishioners. If you are finding that your partner or family are being squeezed out because they fit in the blank spaces in the diary, which compress, then write in some time to spend with them. It is a valid use of your time, and when asked if you are free you are legitimately able to say that you have an appointment in the diary. One curate's wife used to write SEX in the diary, which was fine until he opened it at a church meeting.

Confidentiality

In ministry, all kinds of confidential and sensitive information comes to the curate. In previous posts and situations you may have confided in your spouse or a close friend, but in parish ministry, the church and the community are known to both of you and so confidentiality is critical. If a couple does choose to share everything, this can lead to considerable difficulties, including distorted perceptions and resentments on the part of both the spouse and the parishioners, if they inadvertently discover that the curate's wife or husband knows the intimacies and intricacies of their pastoral needs. Trust may be destroyed; sacramental confession may become impossible. On the other hand, some parishioners will expect that if they have told one partner, both know. Perspective in this requires clear and effective boundaries which are no different from those that people doing other sensitive jobs, like doctors, have to observe. Of course, a curate's spouse may need help in coming to terms with the sense of loss that arises at no longer being their spouse's confidant(e) about everything in the way they once were.

The professional and legal significance of confidentiality and appropriate boundaries in ministry is strongly underlined in the booklet *Guidelines for the Professional Conduct of the Clergy*, and is well worth quoting here:

> 3.11   A person seeking pastoral guidance and counsel from the clergy has the right to expect that the clergy person concerned will not pass on to a third party confidential information so obtained, without their consent or other lawful authority.

> 3.12   Unless otherwise agreed, the clergy are accordingly not at liberty to share confidential information with their spouses, family or friends.

Guidelines 3.13–3.15 contain further important advice about pastoral confidentiality and support.[5]

Spiritual development

Creating a rhythm of life that is supportive is as much about spiritual life as it is about managing work tasks and housework. That might include a daily pattern of work and worship, but also weekly, monthly and annual patterns – even sabbaticals.

Some people find a monthly quiet day helpful.

Whether you need a rule of life, retreats, quiet days, study, training, or a cell group, find patterns that work for you. Find somewhere to pray. That may be in the home, in the church, or even in the park. Your spiritual development will underpin your ministry, and investment in it is a key part of your vocation.

Depending on their tradition, curates have different experiences and expectations of asking others to pray for them, or praying with others. For those with a spiritual director in religious life, it is possible to ask the community to pray for you. Others might seek a prayer partner, either locally or someone they can talk with on the telephone who will pray for them. Neglecting this part of life is as costly as overspending on an overdraft.

Leisure

An ordinand recently confided that his moving into ministry was a challenge for his wife because his work was moving into the house and his job would involve her having a public role. It's inevitable that you'll meet parishioners at the school gate, in the pub and in the supermarket. Is that leisure or an evangelistic opportunity?

Mark Greene from the London Institute of Contemporary Christianity defines work as 'all the things we have to do to maintain our lives' – so it includes ironing, mowing the lawn, doing our taxes, etc. – everything we have to do before we stop for a day and rest and renew ourselves. This begs the question whether clergy – and others – ever stop working.

Recovery or recreation?

An academic study on the value of active and passive leisure has found that those who engage in active leisure – walking, hang-gliding, painting, soccer, etc. – have a significantly better mental and physical well-being than those who have passive leisure or simply recovery time. Active leisure is a great opportunity to get involved in non-church activities and meet people outside the parish. Spending time with others can offer a more realistic view of the parish than if it's the only local activity in which you are involved. One curate takes his son to all the local football team's home games. A season ticket means he has to go because he has spent the money, and it is good for him to spend time away from the workplace with his son.

The Great Commission to work for Christ must be set within the overall context of God's command to stop and to rest. Clergy can be just as prone to becoming workaholics as anyone else in the parish. It's important that ministry does not take over your life. Days off are not just for getting on with jobs that have not been done in the rest of the week; they are about recreation – which may mean getting out of the parish. If you're too tired to do anything on your day off, you need to look at the rest of the week, and find ways of restoring a sustainable rhythm. If there is overspill every week, a diarized catch-up afternoon once a week may be one way of coping with the extra tasks. Days off are also important to partners or close friends as something they can look forward to as being for them as well. Don't let them slip.

Friends and community

As we saw in Chapter 4, ordained ministry brings with it a public role in the parish. Often the people who knock at your door during the first few weeks you are in a new parish will not be the people who end up as your friends. As we have seen, there are pros and cons to having good friends in the parish/congregation, and mixed views about whether this is appropriate or not. However, in the context of how we spend our leisure time, perhaps it is enough simply to observe the following: everyone has friends who inspire, friends to have a good time with, and friends who drain. When time to socialize is at a premium, spend that precious time with the people you really want to be with.

Money

The love of money may be the root of all evil, but ignoring money issues can cause major problems for clergy and bring anxiety and concern.

Whatever curates have earned in their previous working lives, the stipend is likely to be very different. Of course, it comes with accommodation and other allowances, but you will need to manage the transition to a different mode of financial affairs well.

Probably for the first time, your income will not be required to pay rent or mortgage payments on the house where you'll be living. Be clear from the outset about what is paid for by the church/diocese, and what is paid for by you. Making a budget can be a helpful way of allocating money for cars, food, holidays, etc. It can be helpful to open a second account and pay a standing order each month to cover bills such as car insurance, servicing, holidays, phone bills, etc. It's good to keep giving. Many people split their giving between the church within which they are ministering and other places.

It may be that the stipend doesn't meet the budget. Many dioceses now organize occasional courses on financial planning. These cover matters such as income tax, investments and long-term planning, pensions and housing. Of course, clergy with a stipend, no other income and (very often) a family to support have little room for financial manoeuvre, but there are charities available to help with particular needs: archdeacons or other church authorities can usually advise on these. These clergy charities are grant-giving bodies which might provide a grant for a priest with a gifted child who wants to have music lessons, for example (The Sons of the Clergy Corporation[6]), or might provide funds for a holiday (The Friends of the Clergy Corporation[7]). Don't be put off using them because of a fear of accepting 'charity'. Stipends don't allow for luxuries, and these bodies are there to support you. Some dioceses also operate a discretionary funding scheme.

Help with credit and debt problems

It is easy gradually to slip into debt in order to fund one-off items and unanticipated expenses; but any level of persistent debt, especially on credit cards, needs tackling as soon as possible before it gets out of control, and help should also be available for this.

Whether you have minor problems or your finances are massively over-committed, the sooner issues are faced, the easier it will be to sort them out. All churches have structures of some kind for dealing with difficult and delicate issues among ministers. Most now have confidential counselling available to help ministers and their families. This is separate from structures of management. Many too have sources of financial help for clergy in difficulties, sometimes administered confidentially through the archdeacon.

There can be a particular problem for spouses who are aware of problems their partner is having but are afraid of damaging the minister's situation if they ask for the help which their partner is unwilling or unable to seek. There's no easy answer to this, but a spouse has every right to find help to deal with the situation in which they find themselves, and to use confidential services in order to do so.

Don't be afraid to ask for help. Pride conspires with problems to create disasters. The ability to ask for help is a sign of maturity, not weakness.

Status

Income and status can be an issue for the ordained minister. Many NSMs, for example, wrestle with their own and their parish's perception of them doing their job as a volunteer. For stipendiary ministers, there has been a shift in the status of clergy. Historically they might have been the most educated person in a parish. In some areas this might still be true; in others, however, a priest might have to live and minister in a parish where he or she is surrounded by well-paid high-flyers.

Where does your value lie? In the workplace it can be as much in the pay packet as in the nature of the job. In the Church, the world's perception is turned on its head as people leave well-paid jobs to serve in ministry. But if others are judging a curate because their car or clothes are better or worse than those of the community they belong to, it can be a jolt to their identity. However much we know that it is our identity in Christ that is important, other people's perceptions can still hurt.

Practicalities

The Church Commissioners' booklet *Your Stipend* deals with many of the practicalities concerning stipends and the clergy remuneration package.[8] The bureaucracy around income and expenses can be complicated, or it can be straightforward – it partly depends on how you keep your records. Some people throw all their financial paperwork and receipts for the last year or so into a drawer to be dealt with later. Others keep a book in which they record mileage and expenses and keep receipts. However disorganized you like to be normally, finding a system that works for you will save you time in the long run.

For those who need help filling in their tax form, colleagues will be able to advise where to find professional financial help from someone who understands clergy tax.

Financial management for the future

Many clergy maintain or buy a second home as an investment for the future or as a bolt hole. For some, this is not a possibility and it is worth knowing that the Church of England's Pensions Board runs The Church's Housing Assistance for the Retirement Ministry (CHARM) scheme which provides assistance for those wishing to buy or rent a property in retirement.

Your health

We've talked about self-management in terms of paying enough attention to all parts of your life so that you are able to fulfil your ministry effectively. Your health is vital to this. Address health concerns when they come up and if you are ill, take time off. Choosing to live on the edge may be heroic but it also carries the risk of falling off!

8

Moving on

Claire Pedrick and Diane Clutterbuck

Every year about 550 clergy move jobs. Dioceses have differing processes for priests moving on, but for many it feels counter-cultural to apply for jobs. How does 'selling' skills and experience fit with the idea of vocation? Many large companies have an effective internal career development structure, but in the Church there is no clear career path. Sometime during the third or fourth year of a curacy, it's time to apply for a new job and go through another selection process. NSMs might also be looking for a new place in which to develop their vocation at this stage of their ministry.

Whether a priest is just completing a curacy or has been ordained for 25 years, the question is still the same: 'What do I do next?' Even if you are asked to apply for a particular job, it's helpful to clarify what you have to offer – not only to communicate to a future parish, but to discern if this is the right job for you. Here are some pointers for reflection and action, backed up by theory, to help you make the transition from a curacy into the next job.

First things first

It's rare to find a curate who is ambivalent about moving on: some are desperate to leave, others are keen to stay longer. Whatever the feelings, the reality is that curates do move on. What did you learn from the last move? Which questions did you ask that were crucial in making the move to where you are now? What do you wish you had asked and never did? Who are the people you should, in hindsight, have talked to about your present appointment when you were considering it?

During the process of initial selection and training, you are likely to have identified particular passions and areas of interest. Tutors, training incumbents and other colleagues may also have identified gifts and skills in feedback. What were they? Leaving a training post is an opportunity for all clergy to explore what God might be calling them to do next. The post of first responsibility is significant, and thought, prayer, and objective support through the process are key to finding the right place. Clergy often need independent help to reflect at this stage of the process since friends, family and colleagues can have well-meaning but hidden agendas that make it difficult for them to give objective advice.

Breadth or depth?

A Chinese proverb says: 'The banks of the Yangtze give it depth, drive and direction.' Once you are clear about where the 'banks', or boundaries, of your ministry are, you can make informed choices. Many curates have found it helpful to explore their 'purpose' before making applications. A purpose statement helps clarify what you have to offer and what kind of post would fit best with your vocation and skills.

Creating a purpose statement can be fun. What would you want a prospective churchwarden to know about you? Say it in no more than three or four sentences. A purpose statement will clarify and refine what you think about who you are, what you are looking for and what you can bring to a post. It helps to identify jobs that resonate well with your vocation and will nurture and inspire you, while being clear about what you offer enables a possible new parish to discern the right person for their post. Laurie Beth Jones's *The Path* offers tools and ideas to help you develop a purpose statement.[1] It is worth investing time and prayer in this process. A clear understanding of purpose opens up opportunities you might not have considered otherwise and narrows down the right areas to consider. Some clergy involve their spiritual director, work consultant or coach in this process.

Another way of discerning your purpose is to spend five minutes with pen and paper and writing down everything that comes into your head about your ministry – without stopping to think in detail. After five minutes, stop. Read what you've written and highlight any significant areas. Helpful questions to ask include: How does the next phase of ministry fit with what has gone before? What are you moving towards? What is your purpose for your ministry? What do you believe God is calling you to do? Don't think too small – and don't think too big.

Having one eye on the future is another important tool in the discernment process. Clergy interested in theological education, for example, are well advised to seek a post of first responsibility in a parish where they can make links with a theological college or ministerial training scheme. This can help develop skills, experience and networks as a springboard for future applications, or confirm that theological education may not be the right way forward.

Which way forward?

Application and selection processes are a valuable way of gathering suitable applicants and discerning whether the priest is the right person for the job and whether the job is the right opportunity for the priest.

Possible new jobs need to be narrowed down – you can't apply for them all. At critical decision points, the value of a good support structure cannot be underestimated, and prayer, retreats, quiet days and spiritual directors can all be enormously helpful. Many people have friends, former colleagues or clergy who will act as mentors and offer wise counsel. It can be valuable to check out decisions and discern the way forward in this way.

Some make decisions by gathering copious quantities of information; others decide through intuition, looking at the big picture, focusing on relationships and connections between facts. How you make your choice is between you, the people you trust to help you and God, but eventually you have to commit to a particular post. (See also the section on 'Vocation and guidance' in Chapter 3.)

Preparing to apply for a job

Check out job adverts for at least two to three months before making any applications. It can be valuable to circle or clip those that inspire, whether because of location or the wording of the advert. Lay these out on a table or in a scrapbook, and look out for themes. This exercise can uncover extraordinary links and reveal to you what you are really interested in, all of which may be a valuable part of the discernment process. Looking more broadly, it raises other questions, such as: Where does this fit with my sense of vocation now? Where does it fit with the sense of vocation that brought me into ordained ministry?

This preparation time is also an opportunity to look at advertisements for other kinds of jobs, such as chaplaincy, diocesan jobs and theological education.

Assessing your strengths

It is tempting to launch into filling in forms straightaway, but gathering some facts first will save time in the long run and be a way to explore whether a job is worth applying for. Ask yourself questions like:

- What are my gifts?
- What skills do I have from previous working situations?
- What areas do I want to develop?

- What skills have I gathered during my curacy that I can transfer to my post of first responsibility?

- What am I good at?

- What have I learned from this curacy?

If you had a variety of work experience prior to ordination, making a list of all previous jobs (paid and unpaid) will also be helpful. All these things will have developed skills and characteristics that make you the person you are today. I once had a summer job at a Christian centre that involved scrubbing floors, and scrubbing them again after 200 children had tramped mud through. It was dreadful, but it taught me how to serve, and although it's not on my CV, it has influenced my perception of leadership.

Take a large sheet of paper or open up a new computer file and brainstorm onto the page. Think about questions like: What can I do? What can I do well? Include skills gained before ordination, perhaps as a parent, and skills gathered from leisure activities. It might help to group them under headings like:

Communication

Teaching

Working with people – groups and teams

Working with people – one-to-one/pastoral

Working with meetings and church structures

Managing people

Managing money

Managing information

Technical skills, e.g. carpentry, clowning, calligraphy, etc.

Other skills.

Does this list begin to describe what you can do and what you are good at? If not, what is missing? Underline those skills or areas you would like to develop. (Some people find this task difficult and need to enlist the support of a trusted friend to help dig deeper.)

Whether a job is parish-based or not, interviewers will always be looking for a person who has a good balance of skills and experience. A curate must be able to answer questions like: What can you do? What have you to offer this parish/benefice/post that will equip you to be our vicar/rector/priest-in-charge/team vicar?

In order to help the quest for the right job, skills need to be specific, quantified and drawn from experience.

Finding a post

Take heart! Moving from a curacy to a post of first responsibility is likely to be the simplest move you will make in the course of your ministry as the timing is decided for you. It is both inevitable and in the public domain. Before you do anything else it is important to talk with your training incumbent and your bishop. There is plenty of support within Church structures for curates moving into a post of first responsibility, but the responsibility to make things happen lies with you.

There is no laid-down process for this move. You can look in the Church press, respond to adverts or talk to the bishop of another diocese. The Clergy Appointments Adviser (CAA) is based in London and will work with you and help you find a suitable post.[2] Book an appointment as soon as you are sure you are ready to move on. The CAA circulates to the dioceses a list of clergy looking for jobs. Don't put your name onto the CAA list of clergy looking for an appointment until you are ready to move – discuss the best timing for this with the CAA. The CAA also makes contacts with other patrons, including the Crown and the Lord Chancellor's Ecclesiastical Patronage Secretaries.

Some patrons of benefices hold a list of people who are looking for a new post that they will draw on when a vacancy occurs – for example, the Evangelical Patronage Consultative Committee holds a register of clergy looking for a move, which is administered by the Church Pastoral Aid Society.[3] The register is circulated monthly to the trustees of all the member trusts: CPAS Patronage Trust; Martyrs Memorial; Church of England Trust; Church Trust Fund Trust; Simeon's Trust; The Hyndman Trust; Church Patronage Trust; Peach Trust; Church Society; Oxford Churches Trust; Reformation Church Trust; Intercontinental Church Society.

Locally, archdeacons know of posts about to become vacant, as does the clergy grapevine.

Other forms of ministry

The *Church of England Yearbook* contains a helpful section on chaplaincies, including chaplains in higher education and in the forces.[4]

Hospice and hospital chaplains' vacancies are not organized centrally and are all advertised.

School chaplaincies are advertised in the Times Educational Supplement[5] and sometimes in the *Church Times*. School chaplains are often required to teach some RE as well.

Theological education posts are usually advertised in the Church press.

The informal route

Whether formal or informal, most curates have networks – friends from theological college or course, Forward in Faith, Reform, New Wine, Society of Catholic Priests, etc. Discussing a job search with such contacts can open up new possibilities in other areas.

Assessing potential posts

With a plethora of potential jobs and a limited amount of time available, narrowing down applications and discerning the right way forward can be a challenge. An early glance through job adverts will have begun to offer clues about what feels comfortable and what does not. The person and parish profiles that job descriptions carry give some idea of the kind of person the parish is looking for: talking with a training incumbent or a more senior priest can enable a potential applicant to begin to read between the lines of these documents. Similarly, making discreet enquiries of those you know can bring in additional information – and there's always the grapevine.

Other sources of information that can help with research about a post include:

Crockford's Clerical Directory

web sites

quinquennial reports

church accounts

personal contacts (skim through address books)

a visit to the area and the church

taking a friend who can ask objective questions

sending a spy!

The person profile provided by the parish is likely to list 'essentials' and 'desirables'. How do these fit with what you have to offer? Where are the gaps and mismatches and how important are they?

Making an application

Many jobs use the Common Application Form (CAF),[6] and it is tempting, and easy, to use this simply to describe what you have done in your curacy. A future parish will be more concerned, however, with what an applicant can do than with what a past post required – they are not always the same thing.

The CAF asks what you do in your present appointment. For those whose skills range beyond their present post, it's important to know both what they are and how to communicate them on a prescriptive application form. It can be very helpful to download a copy of the CAF as soon as you start to think about making a move, and reflect carefully on the answers you will give.

Other questions on the CAF ask about:

- Your career before ordination: this gives you the opportunity to list previous posts and also include transferable skills that you bring to a new post.

- Your responsibilities within the wider Church. Openness and involvement outside the parish demonstrate a willingness to learn and collaborate. If your experience in this area is rather limited, this might be the time to consider whether you could get involved in the community, deanery or diocese, make a contribution and gain experience.

- Continuing ministerial education (other than POT). The subject of lifelong learning was explored in Chapter 6, but as you scan for possible jobs for now or for the future, think about what kinds of training courses might enhance and develop your skills.

- Publications. For those seeking academic posts, publications are important. Are you applying for a post where it will be possible to write for publication? Who are the key people in your network who can help you in this area?

- Churchmanship tradition. The CAF asks what theological traditions have shaped your ministry. With which do you feel most at ease today? Brainstorm what you want to say about your spiritual journey, and then ask the question: What do I want a parish where I am called to know about this? A churchwarden or friend might have useful insights in this area.

- Activities outside the church – in the community, other interests and hobbies. A friend or colleague may remember things you have overlooked. Do you have skills that could benefit a future parish/job that can be listed here? The diocese that advertised for an e-vicar would be looking for IT/cyber skills, for example.

- Your reasons for applying for the post. What skills will it develop? What other skills and experiences do you bring that have not so far been mentioned? Why do you believe that this might be the right job for you?

The nature of the CAF underlines the dilemma of any selection process. It asks the questions the parish/job would like answered. This may differ, or certainly be less, than an applicant wants to tell them. For that reason, a good understanding and recall of skills and experience both supports the application and interview process and offers a further opportunity to discern whether this is the way God is leading you. Many curates have been challenged at interviews by simple questions about their skills which have floored them, because either they cannot remember or they have insufficient evidence for what they say they can do.

The advantage of the CAF is that biographical data only needs to be filled in once for all applications, and that can be done in advance. This means that you can then pay more attention to the areas that relate specifically to the job you are applying for. If you have prepared thoroughly, the investment of time and energy you have put into understanding and articulating your skills and experience will enable you to give succinct and relevant answers to the questions on the application form. Each form must be tailored carefully to the job description and person profile supplied by the parish. Bullet points can be used to make a more concise presentation.

Interviews

Investment in interview preparation enables candidates to feel relaxed and confident. Looking back on previous interview experiences can draw out clues as to what needs to be in place for an interview to go well. Preparing for an interview is as important as filling in the application form, and should take as much time. Good preparation is about clarity, not about spin. One curate who came across at first as a rather weak and vulnerable person but had significant inner strength developed the strategy of taking someone to the interview with him so that he could warm up talking about himself in the car en route!

Managing change and transition

Most people do not resist change as such. Change is a situational shift connected with external circumstances: moving house, starting theological training, getting ordained and starting a new job and so on. Transition, on the other hand, is the emotional and spiritual process people go through in order to come to terms with change. It is an internal process, and it applies whether the changes to our circumstances are ones we are happy about, or ones we would rather not have happened. It is an unavoidable and necessary emotional and spiritual process that we have to live through – like it or not.

Unfortunately, in conversation and in some books about managing change, change and transition are treated as if they are the same thing. It is in recognizing the difference between them that people begin to live through the process of adjusting to the new way of life and finally reach the point where the new place feels 'normal'.

Endings

Every transition begins with an ending – leaving college or a course, being ordained, leaving your curacy all begin with an ending. These endings need to be marked. In order to move on, everyone has to let go of some aspect of their former life. Moving house loses neighbours and a particular pattern of life; at ordination we become a representative person and lose some of our privacy. At the end of a curacy the curate loses the security of having a training incumbent in a supportive role. Failure to identify the losses that change produces is the largest single problem that people and organizations in transition encounter. We need to grieve for our losses and acknowledge the pain of ending, no matter how joyful the reason for moving on may be. Losses need to be named and marked, even celebrated – what else are hen parties, stag nights and baby showers all about?

Jake is now vicar of a small parish and spends all his time off travelling back to the parish where he had his curacy. It's a great way for him and his family to keep in touch with old friends, but it does mean that his leisure time is still spent in a parish setting.

The wilderness

After letting go of the old way of life and celebrating its ending, we move into a no-man's-land between the old reality and the new. It is a confusing place to be. The outward, situational change probably happened quickly: the inward psychological transition happens more slowly. This middle phase of the transition process can last for weeks, months, or even years. People struggle in the state that is neither old nor new – it is a wilderness time when it isn't clear who we are, what we are for or what is real.

This can create a strong desire to go back. It's not unusual for clergy entering a post of first responsibility with excitement and enthusiasm to stop and wonder whether they have made the right move. But the old life has gone. There is often a compulsion to escape.

But the way back is barred, so the temptation then is to cut short this part of the transition process and jump quickly to the new beginning. In the life of clergy this can take the form of filling every waking moment with activity, never finding time to think or plan or pray.

Many traditional cultures observe a time of withdrawal to mark the transition from childhood into adulthood. Adolescent boys are taken into the forest by a group of wise elders, traditional links with family and friends are broken, and the former identity of the child is stripped away. This is a 'between place': the old reality has gone but the new has not yet been formed. It is an empty place in life and in the world where the seed of the new self can germinate.

In our postmodern society this time of withdrawal has been lost. The temptation is to fill any empty time and place with activity. There needs to be a time of withdrawal at moments of major transition: this is why retreats before ordination are an important part of the shift into ordained ministry. At other times we may not go on a formal retreat, but we need to give ourselves space to allow the internal transition to happen — by walking the hills, sailing a boat on a lake, listening to music or sitting in a quiet place, perhaps.

Moving on is a daunting and exciting time. Support is available during the process if you look for it. Whether you need help to find posts or some assistance from a coach, make sure you take advantage of all the resources at your disposal to find the right place for the next move. You probably won't know what's right until you begin to look. Trying parishes on for size is a good idea, but the emotional cost of doing this can be considerable — hence the value in doing some 'catalogue shopping' from job adverts before you start.

As you will already know from your experience of finding a parish for your first curacy, the process of discernment is by no means scientific. You will be looking for a sense of fit combined with a sense that you are following God's calling. Absolute assurance about the rightness of a decision is, of course, rare. Sometimes you have to take the plunge, live in the new parish — and with your decision — and hang on in there for some time before the rightness of the move becomes clear.

Epilogue

John Witcombe

The world is changing rapidly – and so, therefore, is the Church. This is not the first time the Church has been faced with major cultural changes, and neither will it be the last. The ministry that the Church needs has deep roots but a slender flexibility, to find new shapes to express God's love in each emerging context.

Training today for the land of tomorrow

Changing shapes for ministry suggest changing times for ministers. How can we train people for such a rapidly moving context? What is right for a contemporary expression of ministry in one year seems doomed to hopeless irrelevance only five years down the line.

There are two popular responses to this challenge – responses that can find themselves set against each other. One is to make 'relevance' the yardstick and move towards a 'problem-based learning' method of training in which application is the key. The danger of this may be that foundational disciplines are not sufficiently grasped to enable their application in hitherto unforeseen circumstances. The other, traditional approach to training has been to give a thorough grounding in the theory, on the assumption that its application can be worked out as the minister moves into post. The danger of this approach is that neither students nor ministers may ever adequately make connections between the theory they have learnt and the ministerial context in which they are called to serve, and simply revert to unreflective patterns of practice which they inhabited before entering formal training.

It is probably clear that these two models, the 'workshop' and the 'academy', represent a false dichotomy. Both have their place: the foundational disciplines of biblical study, doctrine, liturgy and spirituality need to be allied to a practical theology which, in demonstrating contemporary praxis, demonstrates and trains students in the underlying principles of reflective practice which can be reinterpreted in every context.

New patterns of training which will encompass everything from the early years of exploring vocation to the years immediately following ordination, drawing them into an integrated whole, are now being developed in the Church of England.[1] This should make it easier to respond to the ever-increasing content of training with a more manageable programme that will enable students to make connections between their study and their ministry in ways that will ultimately breathe life into the Church through the dynamic of genuine praxis.

It is in a lively, and practically relevant, theological environment that new ways of being church will emerge that have integrity with both past and present expressions whilst at the same time expressing God's mission for the future. Investment in this theological resource (akin to a business research and development section) in both time and money is essential to the future of the Church in this country.

Ministers for the Church or the Church for the ministers?

Throughout this book we have explored the relationship between the institution of the Church's ordained ministry and the men and women who embody that ministry in their own particular way. The one shapes the other – for good or ill. There is a responsibility on those in national leadership in the Church to ensure that those who are in local leadership are adequately resourced, cared for, encouraged and challenged in the exercise of their ministry. There is a responsibility on those working locally to ensure that they continue to make their best contribution to the work of the whole.

This book has emerged from a conviction that more work needs to be done to ensure that the newly ordained are enabled both to make their fullest contribution for today, and to lay good foundations for the future. That work will be done in part by the national Church but in large part by the regional and local church, and most especially in the partnership between training incumbent and curate. Curates are precious in God's sight: they are also precious resources for the Church, and need to have their lives and their gifts cherished and nurtured – both by themselves and by others with responsibility for them.

Changing roles

The day of the individual minister who holds all things together is moving towards its sunset. Those who are ordained in the next few years will have no choice but to develop strong skills in team work: collaborative ministry is one of the key motifs of this book. It would be wrong to assume that collaboration makes life easier – but it does make it more effective and more fully human. Within this context it will be more important than ever that the ordained have a realistic understanding of their own gifts, their strengths and weaknesses, and how these enable them to find their place within emerging ministry teams. The national Church needs to continue to develop good personnel practice with regard to the precious resources it has in its ordained clergy, helping them to play the parts to which they are suited and called, and not expecting them to be something they're not.

Future trainers – future church

Many of those reading this book will, in a few years' time, be training curates themselves! We hope that their reflection upon their own training will inform, but not restrict, the patterns that they in turn will use. We hope that they will remember the strengths, and have come to terms with the weaknesses, of their own training before beginning to work with others – revisiting personal notes from one's own early years in ministry should be an essential part of preparing to train others.

Those who are being ordained today will soon find themselves leading and shaping the Church's ministry. What will the Church look like under their leadership? Will they listen to the voices of those who have gone before them, of those who will come after them – and to the voices of those who are not ordained, who are outside the Church altogether? Will they listen to God's voice amongst and within these others, calling them to faithful service that looks to the future with the perspective of the past? Will they feel it is their duty to stand firm whilst all around them changes, or will they be ready to find new forms of expressing God's love in each generation?

The answer must lie, at least in part, in the early years of ministry – and so it is to these years that we offer this book, but with our eyes looking beyond them, in hope, to the future.

Notes

Chapter 1 Vocation, discernment and selection

1 See Ministry Division web site at: www.cofe-ministry.org.uk

2 See web site as in note 1 above.

3 Certain aspects of the selection conference (as it has been known) and the criteria for selection are under review and are likely to change in September 2005.

Chapter 2 The context of ministry

1 CHRISM is the National Association of Christians in Secular Ministry (www.chrism.org.uk).

2 Some characters may be based on real people but names and details have been changed.

3 The term Ordained Local Minister (OLM) has been used since 1998 (previously the term 'Local Non-Stipendiary Minister' [LNSM] or 'Local Ordained Minister' [LOM] was used).

4 The age difference is typical, though of course the genders may differ!

5 This is an increase of 10 per cent on the previous year. Currently there are 18 training schemes (*The Church of England Year Book*, Church House Publishing, 2004).

6 Robin Greenwood writes that the ordination of OLMs cannot be seen 'in isolation from a ministry team that exists to enable the mission and ministry of the whole of the local church' (Robin Greenwood, *The Ministry Team Handbook*, SPCK, 2000, p. 68). However, local ministry can flourish without OLM and some dioceses discourage the 'calling out' of OLMs until a team has been established for two or three years.

7 A diocese with a well-established scheme might expect to include between one-third and one-half of its parishes in this category.

8 A. M. Ramsey, *The Christian Priest Today*, SPCK, 1972, p. 105.

9 *The Structure and Funding of Theological Education Report* raises interesting questions about regional training in the future.

10 Many of the 'elderships' and other structures that have involved lay people in leadership during recent years have simply replaced the 'omnicompetent vicar' with an 'omnicompetent team'. For the average church member, the latter can be even more disempowering than the former.

11 *laos* = both clergy and laity.

12 Many new ways of being church are emerging at present. Some of these use the language of collaboration whilst leadership remains hierarchical (sometimes male-dominated), exclusive, controlling and secretive.

13 In 1968 a case was made for an 'auxiliary pastoral ministry', closely resembling what we now call OLM but leading instead to the development of national NSM. The Tiller Report (*A Strategy for the Church's Ministry*, Church Information Office, 1984) observed that the Church had possibly been looking for ordination candidates in the wrong places! The Church was slow to face the tough issues that the report raised.

14 *Stranger in the Wings*, ABM Policy Paper No. 8, Church House Publishing, 1998, p. 15; chapter 3, pp. 27ff. The acceptance of this report by General Synod in 1999 was the point at which OLM became 'respectable'!

15 Several dioceses do not have OLMs but encourage auxiliary ministry under another name. Sometimes this is similar in ethos, sometimes it is not because it reinforces traditional patterns, particularly when the collaborative context is missing.

16 Roland Allen, *Missionary Methods in St Paul's Time or Ours?*, Lutterworth Press, 1968, pp. vi, 100–4, 151–3, 157–60.

17 In a similar way the 'diaconal' role, also often associated with specifically authorized persons, in local ministry terms belongs to the whole team whose responsibility it is to enable the serving ministry of the whole church.

18 There is an interesting parallel with the early biblical distinction between 'presbyter' and 'bishop', a role which evolved into that of 'overseer'. Today 'local pastors' work under the supervision of 'chief pastors', not only in relationships between diocesan bishops and incumbents but also between local priests and their stipendiary colleagues, who take on an increasingly 'episcopal' role.

19 It is accepted that training for stipendiary ministers is usually a preparation for the 'oversight' ministry of incumbency. Steven Croft points to the need to re-evaluate the concepts behind *presbuteros*, *diakonos* and *episkopos* (*Ministry in Three Dimensions*, Darton, Longman & Todd, 1999, pp. 39–41).

20 Our use of the word 'priest' today has its roots both in the New Testament 'presbyter' and the Old Testament concept of priest as mediator.

21 The Porvoo Statement summarizes this by saying that all the baptized are involved in interceding for the Church and the world, so demonstrating the corporate priesthood of the whole people of God. Porvoo Statement, Council for Christian Unity, 1993.

22 There is a consensus among writers from different backgrounds that, whilst the whole Church has the potential to express what God is doing, we still need 'representative persons'. 'Priests' today are people who enable the Church to fulfil its mediating role. They derive their priesthood from the corporate priestliness of the whole people of God, rather than vice versa (Robin Greenwood, *Transforming Priesthood*, SPCK, 1994, pp. 149–50). See also Lesslie Newbigin, *The Gospel in a Pluralist Society*, SPCK, 1989; Hans Küng, *The Church*, Search Press, 1968, pp. 382–3.

23 Vincent Donovan, *Christianity Rediscovered*, SCM Press, 1987, pp. 147–50.

24 Donovan, *Christianity Rediscovered*, pp. 143–9, 151–2, 158.

25 Stewart C. Zabriskie, *Total Ministry*, Alban Institute, 1997, pp. 27ff. Lichfield Diocese uses the phrase 'sacramental identity' to describe the personal quality that is the primary 'qualification' for being a 'representative person'.

26 Ironically, the same fear was expressed 30 years ago about NSMs. Perhaps OLMs are in third place!

27 OLMs are licensed to their own parish (though 'local' is often interpreted as team or group or deanery), though they are only slightly more restricted than most parish clergy who only minister outside their licence by invitation. If regular help is required in a neighbouring parish, the stipendiary, not the OLM, would be expected to go, but occasional visits are quite normal.

28 Most dioceses have an agreed process by which an OLM of several years' standing can transfer. However, an essential part of the early discernment process is to check the desirability, for both candidate and parish, that this ministry be localized and long-term.

29 The phrase 'hinge leadership' has been used to describe the uncomfortable role of being at home in more than one culture, holding the tension between the best of what is old and new (Gerard Kelly, *Get a Grip on the Future*, Monarch Books, 1999, p. 236). The Tomorrow Project referred to 'entrepreneurial' stipendiary clergy in 'specialist jobs' (Moynagh/Worsley:2000:109).

Chapter 3 Getting started: training and finding a curacy

1 For details see www.stjohns_nottm.ac.uk

2 Paul Ballard and John Pritchard, Practical Theology in Action, SPCK, 1996, p. 10.

3 See the Ministry Division web site at: www.cofe-ministry.org.uk

4 See Ministry Division Code of Procedure (revised February 2004) available on the Ministry Division web site (n. 2 above).

5 Wesley Carr, *Handbook of Pastoral Studies*, SPCK, 1997, p. 158.

6 *Studying Congregations: A New Handbook*, ed. Nancy T. Ammerman and others, Abingdon, 1998.

7 See 'Curacy Appointments', from the Bishop's Committee for Ministry Guidelines, 1999. A useful resource sheet which offers further suggestions for questions to ask at the interview about both the church and the area is 'Situations Vacant', available from the Church Pastoral Aid Society, Athena Drive, Tachbrook Park, Warwick CV34 6NG.

8 See Sue Walrond Skinner, *Double Blessing: Partners in Marriage and Ministry: A Practical Guide for Husbands and Wives Engaged in Professional Ministry Together, and for the Advisers*, Ministry Division, 1995.

9 The text of the service called 'The Ordinal' may be found on the Ministry Division web site. It is due to be updated in 2005.

Chapter 4 Inner self: the 'being' of being a curate

For further study on issues of the formation of identity, personhood and role, see Alistair I. McFadyen, *The Call to Personhood: A Christian Theory of the Individual in Social Relationships*, Cambridge University Press, 1990.

2 *The Penguin Dictionary of Psychology* defines the word 'role' in terms of 'any pattern of behaviour involving certain rights, obligations and duties which an individual is expected, trained and, indeed, encouraged to perform in a given social situation. In fact, one may go so far as to say that a person's role is precisely what is expected of him or her by others and ultimately, after the role has been thoroughly learned and internalised, by the person him or herself.' We shall go on to explore expectations in the context of various relationships in Part 2 of this chapter.

3 It is interesting and informative to ask candidates for ordination to do a similar exercise using the heading 'A priest is someone who …'. This quickly reveals something of their theology of priesthood!

4 It is worth pointing out that these questions of role and identity are worth revisiting from time to time throughout a person's ordained ministry, and not just in the early years after ordination.

5 For an examination of this dilemma, see Vanessa Herrick and Ivan Mann, *Jesus Wept: Reflections on Vulnerability in Leadership*, Darton, Longman & Todd, 1998.

6 It is worth underlining the value of the Christmas 'round robin' letter in this regard.

7 See John N. Collins, *Deacons and the Church: Making Connections between Old and New*, Gracewing/Moorhouse Publishing, 2002.

8 Rowan Williams, 'Vocation (1)', in *Open to Judgement: Sermons and Addresses*, Darton, Longman & Todd, 1994, p. 174.

9 Williams, 'Vocation (1)', p. 176.

Chapter 5   Public ministry

1 David J. Schlafer, *Your Way with God's Word: discovering your distinctive preaching voice*, Cowley Publications, 1995.

2 An excellent resource is David Day, *A Preaching Workbook*, Lynx, 1998.

3 Mark Greene, various articles and *The Three-Eared Preacher: A Listening Tool for Busy Ministers*, 1998 (available from London Bible College).

4 Examples may be found in *A Manual of Anglo-Catholic Devotion*, Canterbury Press, 2001, pp. 87ff., which may need adapting for local use, or The Episcopal Church of the United States of America's *Book of Common Prayer*, Seabury Press, 1979, p. 447, which I have used for many years.

Chapter 6 Maturing into your vocation

1 David Lyall and John Fosket, *Helping the Helpers*, SPCK, 1988, p. 33.

2 *Mind the Gap: Integrated Continuing Ministerial Education for the Church's Ministers*, Church House Publishing, 2001, p. 1.

3 See *Mind the Gap*; *Beginning Public Ministry*, ABM Ministry Paper No. 17, 1998, which gives detailed guidance on ministerial formation and personal development of clergy in the first four years after ordination; *Stranger in the Wings*, ABM Policy Paper No. 8, GS 532, which was a major review of ordained local ministry that included recommendations for CME.

4 This is work in progress. A working party is currently planning the implementation of recommendations of the Hind Report, *Formation for Ministry within a Learning Church*, GS 1496, Church House Publishing, 2003. The main conclusions of this report are helpfully summarized in booklet form. The Regional Training Partnerships are intended to enable a more careful integration of the training process from pre-selection, through the ordination courses and into the first years of ordained ministry.

5 The failure to recognize and value hard-earned skills and experience is a fairly common source of pain and anger for the newly ordained. One of the priorities in the early meetings between a new curate and their training incumbent must be to identify existing areas of competence in which they are confident. It is important that these are recognized, and their appropriate contribution valued, alongside the learning of new competencies in the life of ministry.

6 OLMs gain their primary support from being part of a locally mandated team.

7 Archbishop Rowan Williams in an interview with Paul Handley, *Church Times*, 6 December 2002. He was replying to a question about what it means to belong to the Church at this time.

8 Eugene Petersen, *The Contemplative Pastor*, William B. Eerdman, 1994.

9 *Affirmation and Accountability: Practical Suggestions for Preventing Clergy Stress, Sickness and Ill Health Retirement*, Society of Mary and Martha, 2002, has been an influential report that offers a series of important recommendations for the care and nurture of clergy. See also www.sheldon.uk.com.

10 The National Retreat Association, Central Hall, Bermondsey Street, London SE1 3UJ. Tel: 020 7357 7736.

Chapter 7 Self-management

1 *Guidelines for the Professional Conduct of the Clergy*, Church House Publishing, 2004.

2 For more information about MBTI® and for a list of Registered MBTI® consultants in your area, contact OPP Ltd, Elsfield Hall, 15–17 Elsfield Way, Oxford OX2 8EP.

3 The Service for the Ordination of Priests, *The Alternative Service Book 1980*.

4 Mark Forster, *How to Get Everything Done and Still have Time to Play*, Hodder & Stoughton.

5 *Guidelines for the Professional Conduct of the Clergy* (see n. I above).

6 The Sons of the Clergy Corporation, I Dean Trench Street, Westminster, London SWIP 3HB. Tel: 020 7799 3696.

7 The Friends of the Clergy Corporation, 27 Medway Street, Westminster, London SWIP 2BD. Tel: 020 7222 2288. Fax: 020 7233 1244. Email: focc@btinternet.com. See http://www.friendsoftheclergy.org.

8 *Your Stipend*, Church Commissioners, Millbank, London SWIP 3JZ.

Chapter 8 Moving on

I Laurie Beth Jones, *The Path*, Hyperion, 1988.

2 Clergy Appointments Adviser, Cowley House, 9 Little College Street, London, SWIP 3SH. Tel: 020 7898 1898.

3 The Patronage Secretary, Church Pastoral Aid Society, Athena Drive, Tachbrook Park, Warwick CV34 6NG. Tel: 01926 458461. Email: patronage@cpas.org.uk.

4 *The Church of England Yearbook*.

5 Go to http://www.tes.co.uk/

6 The CAF can be downloaded from http://home.clara.net/caa/commonap.html.

Epilogue

I The Hind Report – Formation for Ministry within a Learning Church: The Structure and Funding of Ordination Training (GS 1496), Church House Publishing, 2003.

Index

Note: Where two sequences of notes appear on the same page, they are distinguished by the addition of 'a' or 'b' following the note number.